HORRIBLE BRITISH TRUE CRIME

TRUE CRIME

VOLUME THREE

Ben Oakley

Look for more in the Orrible British True
Crime Series!

OUT NOW!

Orrible British True Crime Volume 3

From the 19th Century to the 21st, a bonanza collection of British true crime stories covering murder, serial killers, robbery, and a gentleman hacker.

1. The Pottery Cottage Massacre

A violent criminal escaped prison by stabbing two guards, then took an entire family hostage in their rural home before killing four of them, in a case that shocked England.

2. The Royal Navy Serial Killer

A gay Petty Officer in the Royal Navy killed at least two young sailors and has since been suspected of killing up to twenty, in one of Hampshire's worst cases of serial killing.

3. Murder By The Canal

When an abused woman reported her partner to police for assault, she never expected to become instrumental in solving the murder of a young girl twenty years earlier.

4. The House of Blood Murders

An argument between lovers resulted in a triple murder at a house in Glasgow, branded the House of Blood killings, with the ringleader known as the mother of all evil.

5. The Oxford Student Murder

A football fan watched his team win the FA Cup semi-final, then killed his girlfriend, hid the corpse under the floorboards of her house, and weaved an elaborate tale in an attempt to outwit the police.

6. The Ughill Hall Murders

In a double murder that shocked Sheffield, a successful solicitor killed his mistress and her daughter, and left her son for dead, before fleeing to France and threatening to jump off the Amiens Cathedral.

7. The Case of the Green Bicycle Murder

A murder mystery involving a female victim, bloody bird prints, a dead crow, a gun in a canal, a pea-green bicycle, and a 100-year search for the truth, in a case fit for Sherlock Holmes.

8. The Midlands Ripper

A lorry driver with a hatred of women killed two sex workers in Leicestershire, resulting in Operation Enigma that reviewed the unsolved murders of 200 more.

9. Murder in the Red Barn

A sensational 19th Century murder, an illegitimate child, a supernatural dream, a shallow grave, an evil squire, and a red barn, make for one of the most notorious olde English murder cases.

10. The Burglars of Baker Street

A heist involving millionaire moles, underground tunnels, corrupt cops, MI5 censorship, a chicken takeaway, The Sweeney, and a conspiracy theory that reached all the way to the British royal family.

11. The Keyworth Murder

A confident killer murdered a 16-year-old girl and escaped justice for 25 years until advancements in DNA technology captured him, in the first case to be profiled on Crimewatch.

12. The Cage Beneath Monster Mansion

Known as the real Hannibal the Cannibal, Britain's most dangerous prisoner was confined to a specially built glass isolation cage in the basement of one of the country's most notorious prisons.

13. The Black Panther Serial Killer

With over 400 thefts, 19 post office robberies, four murders, and countless assaults to his name, the Black Panther was Britain's most prolific criminal, known for the disturbing death of a kidnapped girl.

14. The Jolly Farmer Explosion

A giant explosion levelled a quaint English pub and left one person dead, but as the rubble was cleared, a survivor was found, and a realisation the explosion was no accident.

15. Gentleman Hacker

A crowd of scientists gathered in London for the first public demonstration of the wireless telegram system, only for a British magician to tap the signal and become the world's first hacker.

The Pottery Cottage Massacre

A violent criminal escaped prison by stabbing two guards, then took an entire family hostage in their rural home before killing four of them, in a case that shocked England.

There have been numerous mass murderers, serial killers, and violent criminals throughout the history of Britain. Many, like Dennis Nilsen, Jack the Ripper, the Dunblane Massacre, and Harold Shipman, are well known.

Then there are those like William Thomas Hughes, who tend to get overshadowed by the more written about infamous names and monikers. His tale involves a life of crime, a prison break, mass murder, a high-speed car chase, and hostage taking.

He was considered so maniacal that when an officer shot him in the head, the bullet appeared to bounce off, making Hughes even wilder. His crimes are somewhat lost to the annals of British true crime but his case is begging to be retold.

From the 12th to 14th of January 1977, Hughes escaped from custody, stabbed two prison officers, took an entire family hostage, killed four of them, kidnapped the sole surviving family member, went on the run, and was hunted down by police before being shot dead.

Antisocial

The village of Eastmoor on the outskirts of Chesterfield town in England, is so small that you could drive through it without even knowing it's there. It's home to sprawling country homes, cottages, and farmland, seated right on the Eastern edge of the Peak District National Park. But it will be forever linked with the crimes committed by Hughes.

Born William Thomas Hughes in 1946 in Preston, Lancashire, he was the first of six children to parents Thomas and Mary. From an early age, he was antisocial, performed poorly at school and was known to bully other children.

There was no seemingly obvious reason as to why Hughes became antisocial, though some suspected that being the eldest of six children, he felt isolated and was able to get away with more while his parents were focused on his younger siblings.

He left school at 15 with low grades and no idea what he wanted to do. As such, he flittered between various dead-end jobs and struggled to hold down any of them, instead preferring a life of crime. As a juvenile, he spent time in youth detention for robbery and violence.

When he was 20, in 1966, he was jailed for the first time for assault but was out within a few months. He married a younger woman while in Preston and had one child with her but the relationship went sour when Hughes became violent towards her and slept with other women.

In March 1976, he left his wife and moved to Chesterfield with his new girlfriend to start afresh but the violence followed, as it inevitably always would. Within a few weeks he was known to have been violent towards his new partner. Then in August of that year, his crimes escalated.

Category C prisoner

In Chesterfield on 21st August 1976, Hughes was out drinking in town when he went to a nightclub and met a young couple. There was an altercation between them and the couple left the club, but Hughes followed them into a nearby park.

He hid in the shadows and watched them have sex behind the public swimming baths. As they were lost in the moment, he crept up behind them and hit the man over the head with a brick multiple times, then dragged the woman to the nearby riverbank and raped her.

The next day, police appealed for information about the incident and many witnesses came forward to state they had seen Hughes leave the club and follow the couple into the park. Fortunately, the couple survived the attack but were left with life-changing injuries.

Hughes was arrested and charged with rape and violent assault, then remanded in custody until a trial date could be set – but that's when it all started to go wrong. When Hughes was transported to HMP Leicester, the police and prison service failed to pass over his previous records.

It meant that Hughes became a Category C prisoner; a low-risk criminal. This was despite the nature of the crimes he was on remand for, and his previous convictions for violence. His previous records, along with a pre-trial report stating Hughes to be of a violent nature were put together but were not forwarded to HMP Leicester until after he had escaped.

While in prison, he told fellow inmates that he was going to escape and head back to Lancashire to kill his ex-wife. One reported it to the guards but it fell on deaf ears. It seemed that the authorities were enabling Hughes without even knowing it.

Violent escape

On 3rd December 1976, while working in the prison kitchen, Hughes stole a boning knife, which is used to cut through the ligaments on raw meat. He managed to hide the knife in his cell despite various searches by the guards.

Then on 12th January 1977, Hughes was scheduled to appear at Chesterfield court for the fifth time since he had been remanded. The previous four times had gone off without a hitch and so the prison guards became lapse with Hughes's security, believing him to be no cause for concern.

There were some unfortunate coincidences that led to the escape. On that fateful day, the weather conditions were bad as heavy snow had fallen across the country. The near 55-mile route had multiple hold-ups and was generally difficult to navigate.

The prison service hired a taxi to take Hughes and two prison officers, Don Sprintall and Ken Simmonds, to the courthouse. Due to the set-up in the taxi, Hughes was only handcuffed to Simmonds by one wrist on the back seat.

Sprintall sat in the passenger seat and spoke to the taxi driver about the conditions. Hughes had already been searched but he had managed to conceal the boning knife in his clothing. With one arm free, Hughes was able to pull off a violent escape.

Due to the length of time the journey was taking, Hughes begged to stop and use a public toilet, where he removed the knife from his clothing. Within moments of getting back into the car, Hughes reached forward and stabbed Sprintall in the back of the neck, splashing blood onto the car window.

Almost immediately, he stabbed Simmonds in the neck, who struggled to stop the flow of blood. Hughes ordered the taxi driver to pull over. He unlocked his handcuffs and dragged the two seriously injured guards out of the car then drove off leaving all three of them on the roadside.

Manhunt

Less than a mile later, and due to the heavy weather conditions, Hughes crashed into a border wall and exited the car, eloping on foot to Beeley Moor, a small village in the Peak District. The prison service and police were made aware of the escape within minutes and emergency services flooded to the location where the guards were bleeding into the snow.

Less than half hour later, the taxi was found by the wall, abandoned. A manhunt got underway led by Chief Inspector Peter Howse, who would later tell his story in a book, describing how the events haunted him for the rest of his life.

Due to the heavy snow, any footprints were covered up quickly, and search dogs failed to pick up a scent. Because the conditions were so severe, Peter and the team believed that Hughes would have hidden in and around Beeley Moor, as it would have been treacherous to walk over the moorland in the other direction.

The team searched over 250 properties within the first few hours and found no sign of Hughes. Peter struggled with resources and wanted to search more properties and locations but simply didn't have the manpower to do so.

A search radius was set up where it was believed Hughes would be, but unbeknownst to Peter and the team, Hughes *had* traipsed over the moorland. After four miles in deadly conditions, Hughes arrived in the village of Eastmoor and chose one property to hide in. Before the police were even looking for him, Hughes had already taken a family hostage.

Pottery Cottage

The Pottery Cottage was originally named Northend Farm and was a working pottery barn for most of its life. In October 1969, Solihull-born grocery shop owners, Arthur Minton, and his wife Amy, retired and sold their business before purchasing Northend farm and moving to Eastmoor.

Along with one of their daughter's, Gillian, and her husband Richard Moran, they set about converting the property into two living units, and proudly renamed the site; Pottery Cottage. Gillian and Richard had adopted a baby girl two years earlier and named her Sarah.

Richard was born in Ireland and served in the Irish Army for a short amount of time before leaving for a sales job where he met Gillian, who was an accountant's secretary.

At the time that Hughes changed their lives forever, all five were living at the cottage. Arthur was 72, Amy, 68, Richard, 36, Gillian, 29, and Sarah, 10. Only one would survive.

At around 10am, Hughes approached Pottery Cottage, freezing and exhausted. After a quick search of the outside of the property, he found two axes in the shed. With one in each hand, he entered the cottage through the back door to find Arthur and Amy preparing vegetables for the evening meal.

He was surprisingly honest and told them he was on the run from police and needed a place to stay only until nightfall when he would leave them alone. He promised not to hurt them but took control of one of their vegetable knifes for good measure.

Psychological games

Hours passed until 3pm when Gillian arrived home from work. Amy told her the truth that Hughes was on the run from police and that he promised not to harm them. Sarah arrived home from school half hour later and was told by Gillian that Hughes's car was broken and he was waiting for help.

It would have been a strange scene with no sign of what was to come. Gillian and her mother made small talk over coffee, Arthur was sat in his armchair watching TV and Sarah was happily running around the house as if nothing was untoward.

Then, at around 6pm, Richard returned home, and Hughes's demeanour changed. When Richard walked through the front door, he saw Hughes holding a knife to his wife's throat. Hughes ordered Richard onto the floor where he tied him up.

Following suit, he restrained Gillian and Amy. Arthur resisted but was eventually tied and gagged. Hughes dragged them into separate rooms, and walked Sarah through to the annex where she was locked in.

On the first night, Hughes made tea for everyone but decided to rape Gillian shortly after. That night, Gillian heard a commotion from the downstairs living room where Arthur had been tied to his armchair. She realised he was being beaten, and less than an hour later, Arthur's cries subsided.

At 7.30am the next morning, a lorry arrived at the cottage on a routine trip to empty the septic tank.

Hughes ordered Gillian to sign the papers or he would kill her family. She noticed that Arthur had been covered with a jacket and couldn't see his face, but Hughes told her he was sleeping, and that Sarah was still asleep in the annex – he was lying.

Discovery of victims

Hughes ordered Gillian to phone her work and Sarah's school to say they were ill, then told Richard to do the same thing for his work. Hughes even made Gillian head to the local shop to get cigarettes and newspapers, and to note where the roadblocks were.

When she returned, she noticed that her father was no longer in the armchair, with Hughes claiming he was back in his own bedroom. On that second day, he untied Amy, Richard, and Gillian, and allowed them to eat and sit at the table. He told them Arthur and Sarah would remain separated from them.

Hughes had planned to leave on the second night but the weather had become worse and the driving conditions were impossible. He decided that as he was in control of the cottage, he would remain for one more night.

The following morning, on the 14th, he ordered Richard and Gillian to go shopping for supplies and they thought about telling the police but were worried what would happen to the family members in the house. They returned to the cottage, and Richard was ordered to go to his place of work and clean out the petty cash, before returning later that evening.

Hughes tied up Richard and Amy again and said he was going to take Gillian as a hostage. When the car wouldn't start, he told Gillian to get help from the neighbours but she told them about the hostage situation and Hughes overheard.

As Gillian got back into the car, she noticed Amy stagger out of the house holding her neck before falling to her back on the frozen ground. Hughes had cut her throat in retaliation for Gillian telling the neighbours.

The neighbours alerted police who arrived at Pottery Cottage around 9pm. Amy was found dead on her back in the garden, partially covered with snow, and her throat cut. When they entered the cottage, they found three more bodies.

Richard had died from knife wounds to the chest and neck, as had Arthur, who had been killed on the first night and covered up by Hughes. But perhaps the most difficult sight was that of 10-year-old Sarah, who had been sexually assaulted then stabbed in the chest and neck. She too, had been murdered on the first night.

Final moments

Realising what had gone down, Chief Inspector Peter Howse called for as much assistance as possible, even involving two Army helicopters but they had to be grounded due to the weather. The police finally spotted Hughes driving the Moran's car.

A high speed car chase ensued that took them across Derbyshire and into Cheshire, which ended when Hughes crashed the car into a garden wall in the tiny village of Rainow, in the valley of the River Dean.

Hughes held an axe to Gillian's head, demanding a new vehicle to escape in. Peter led the negotiations and managed to provide a new vehicle for Hughes but Gillian refused to move, having reached breaking point.

With armed police surrounding him, Hughes saw no way out. He raised the axe, ready to kill Gillian, but Peter jumped through the car window and covered her. It gave time for an armed officer to shoot Hughes in the head.

Hughes staggered back but didn't fall, instead becoming enraged at the headshot. He lifted the axe again and was shot three more times before finally collapsing to the ground. He died of his injuries right there in the snow beside the wall he had crashed into.

His death was notable as the first time that British police has shot dead a fugitive, and the first time an officer from Derbyshire police had shot anyone dead.

One of the worst

An inquiry into the incident criticised many aspects of the case, including search procedures at HMP Leicester, and the lack of information and incomplete records between police and prison departments. The inquiry ended with 17 different recommendations, all of which were accepted and made law by the government.

Despite the police coming under fire for searching a geographically limited area, Peter Howse was recommended for commendation after jumping in front of Gillian to protect her from the axe. He later received the Queen's Commendation Award for Brave Conduct.

Hughes was due to be buried at a cemetery in Chesterfield but outraged locals protested as they didn't want him buried in their town. They threatened to dig up the grave if he was buried there, so authorities decided to cremate him privately.

Prison guards Don Sprintall and Ken Simmonds survived being stabbed in the neck and returned to work soon after. For Gillian, her life changed immeasurably. Hughes had physically and psychologically abused her, playing games in the house telling her that Sarah was alive when she wasn't.

At the funeral of Sarah, Richard, Arthur, and Amy, Gillian had a police escort to keep the intense media pressure off her. Later in 1977, she sold her story to The Daily Mail which was released in eight parts. She never spoke to the media again and remained silent of the nightmare that robbed her of everyone she loved.

Hughes was a career criminal enabled by a system that led to multiple murder. Throughout his life, he raped at least three women, seriously injured four people, killed another four, and tore apart a community. He is one of the worst criminals to have ever walked the streets of Derbyshire and Cheshire, and perhaps, the entire country.

The Royal Navy Serial Killer

A gay Petty Officer in the Royal Navy killed at least two young sailors and has since been suspected of killing up to twenty, in one of Hampshire's worst cases of serial killing.

With 1.9million residents, Hampshire is one of the most densely packed counties in England, with only Kent, West Yorkshire, Greater Manchester, West Midlands, and Greater London topping it out. As such, the county has been home to some of the most brutal crimes.

Perhaps no more so than the case of Allan Michael Grimson, whose name has mostly remained protected from international scrutiny, until now. Though convicted of two murders, it has long been suspected that Grimson killed more, with as many as 20 undiscovered victims.

It wasn't only Hampshire that bore the brunt of his violent campaign, he has been linked to murders as far afield as Gibraltar and New Zealand. Despite being a serial killer, Grimson is believed to be held in an open prison, where he is considered low-risk.

Grimson was a sailor with the Royal Navy and travelled to the far corners of the earth with the service, it was this supposed international anonymity that allowed him to claim the victims of his choosing. He was also known as the '*Frankenstein Killer*', who cut off the ears of his victims and slit their throats with a knife.

The Parkes disappearance

Born in 1958, in North Shields, Northumberland, Grimson dreamed of joining the Navy and as soon as he was old enough, escaped his hometown and enlisted in 1978. Though the two convicted murders took place in the late nineties, he has long been linked to an unexplained disappearance in 1986.

Grimson was serving on the HMS Illustrious, a light aircraft carrier, while it was docked in Gibraltar. Serving with him on the ship at the time was 18-year-old leading seaman Simon Parkes, born in 1968 in Kingswood, Gloucestershire.

In December 1986, the crew of the Illustrious were afforded some welcome shore leave, after having near circumnavigated the world on a tour known as '*Global 86*'. Gibraltar was the last stop before heading back to the ship's home port in Portsmouth, Hampshire.

On 12th December, Parkes was out drinking with shipmates at a pub called the Horseshoe Bar, when he left to find some food, stating he had drunk a little too much. He was seen in another pub nearby shortly after by a witness who claimed he was so drunk he couldn't stand.

When he didn't return to the ship the following morning, he was assumed missing, and a 250-man search team began scouring the areas he had last been seen but no trace of him was found.

Unsolved missing person

At the time, Parkes was considered to have gone AWOL (absent without leave), but there was no basis for him doing so. He had left his passport in his cabin, along with Christmas presents for his family in England, and a special pass for his family to join him dockside when the Illustrious arrived home.

His shipmates confirmed to their superiors and investigators that Parkes was looking forward to returning home and was not the type to have eloped. It wouldn't be until 2001 when Grimson was linked to his disappearance.

After his convictions, it emerged that Grimson was in the Horseshoe Bar and had been seen drinking with Parkes. Grimson was gay, but not openly so, though he was often seen fraternising with other gay men aboard the ship, especially those younger than him.

In 2003, British police flew to Gibraltar and used specialist teams to search the areas where Parkes was last seen, including local cemeteries. In 2005, the BBC aired two investigative programmes looking into Parkes's disappearance, but in both cases, no body was found.

Both the police and the BBC pointed the finger at Grimson, who was then in jail for the two known murders but they couldn't prove he had killed Parkes. In 2019, Hampshire police received an anonymous tip that Parkes was buried in Trafalgar Cemetery in Gibraltar but it was proven to be false.

The Nicholas Wright experience

The disappearance of Parkes, and Grimson's possible involvement has long been suspected to be true, even more so when we look at a surprising link between Parkes and the murders in the next section, one that would have some researchers reaching for their tin foil hats.

In November 1997, Grimson was on a Navy-run fire-fighting course in Portsmouth when he met 18-year-old fellow sailor Nicholas Wright. He took a fancy to the eager youngster and invited him out for drinks in Portsmouth on a regular basis.

By that point, Grimson had achieved the rank of Petty Officer (PO) but used his ever-increasing power to his advantage. He told Wright that he would drive him back to his home in Leicester on the weekends, and Wright didn't refuse, as it meant a free ride home.

Even at that time, Wright's family were suspicious of Grimson's motives, suspecting he wanted more than a friendship with Wright. On 12th December 1997, Wright and Grimson were drinking together in a Portsmouth nightclub and were seen leaving together in the early hours.

Grimson took Wright back to his flat in London Road, North End, where he attempted to kiss him but Wright pushed him away. Grimson took offence at being refused his sexual advances and started punching Wright in the head. Not willing to let his anger die down, he reached for a nearby baseball bat.

He beat Wright into unconsciousness then cut his throat with a kitchen knife. Bizarrely, he sliced off Wright's ear before placing the body in the bathtub and going to bed. He wanted to take body parts for trophies but decided against it.

The next night, Grimson wrapped Wright's body in black bin bags, put him in the boot of his car and drove towards Cheriton village, 20 miles away. Along the way, while dressed in his Navy uniform, he pulled over to talk to a police officer, knowing that Wright was in the back.

The officer had no idea about the body in the boot of the car and Grimson drove on to Cheriton where he buried Wright's body in a shallow grave on a grassy patch beside the A272 road. The body wouldn't be found until one year later.

Grimson was questioned about the disappearance by police and military police but lied his way out of trouble. He later claimed he got a thrill of putting himself in the firing line and said that '*murder was better than sex*'. He referred to the murder as '*the Nicholas Wright experience*'.

Thrill killer

The thrill of the kill had spurred Grimson on to his second confirmed victim, 20-year-old Sion Jenkins, a year later in December 1998. Originally from Newbury, Jenkins had joined the Navy at a young age but decided it wasn't for him and left when he was 19.

Grimson already had his sights set on Jenkins and would frequent the Hogs Head bar in Portsmouth where Jenkins worked after leaving the Navy. On the night of 12th December, Grimson went to Joanna's Nightclub in Portsmouth and met up with Jenkins.

He lured the drunk barman back to his flat where he forced him to perform sexual acts. After punching and threatening him, he raped Jenkins and tied him to the bed. In the morning, Jenkins begged Grimson to let him leave but Grimson had other ideas. He wanted to repeat the thrill of the Wright murder and decided to kill Jenkins.

He reached for the baseball bat and beat Jenkins until he was no longer breathing, crushing his skull in the process. The following night, he dumped the body on a small area of land on the A32 in West Tisted, 24 miles away, and only four miles from where he had buried Wright.

When police investigated the disappearance, Grimson's name kept coming up in witness statements as someone who might have been involved. In late December 1998, 40-year-old Grimson was brought into Portsmouth Police station for an interview, where he confessed to Wright's murder.

Serial killer by nature

Grimson told police where they could find Wright's body. Then, feeling the power afforded to him by his actions, Grimson confessed to Jenkins's murder, which was only considered to be a disappearance at the time.

A day after digging up Wright's body, police were led to where Jenkins had been buried. Grimson was charged with both murders and ultimately went to trial, when in 2001 he was convicted of both and sentenced to 22 years in prison.

The sentence was increased to 25 years by the then Home Secretary, with a side note that he should never be released. Yet, in 2008, his sentence was reduced by three years on appeal, based on his guilty plea, time spent on remand, and a psychological report revealing an undiagnosed personality disorder.

A specialised psychiatrist who had amassed decades of research and had studied 250 other murderers and serial killers, met with Grimson, and later told the media that he was the worst psychopath he had ever come across.

The judge at the trial told Grimson, '*you are a serial killer in nature if not in number. You are a highly dangerous serial killer who killed two young men in horrifying circumstances.*' It was around the time of Grimson's conviction that police began looking into other murders.

12th December

The FBI's definition of a serial killer is the unlawful killing of two or more victims by the same offender in separate events. Britain doesn't have a standard and either tends to use the FBI definition, or three, depending on the police force. This researcher suggests three is the definition within Britain.

And as such, when investigators began looking closer at Grimson's movements, they discovered an eerie link between the two confirmed victims. Both had been killed on 12th December, one year apart. With that in mind, they began to link up Grimson's movements on the same date for every year he was in the Navy.

The 12th of December link was the sole reason Grimson was linked to the Parkes disappearance in Gibraltar. In an unusual twist of fate, Parkes had also gone missing on 12th December and was presumed dead or killed.

With the date theory in place, it was suggested by police that Grimson may have been deliberately killing people on the 12th of December every year since 1978, which meant there could have been at least 20 victims.

It was the date theory that led to the police and the BBC investigating the Parkes disappearance in 2003 and 2005 respectively. When they began tracking Grimson's movements, a team of specialist British detectives landed in New Zealand to look through missing persons reports and unsolved murder files.

Grimson had been in Auckland as a Royal Navy fire instructor for four months between June and September 1998. One unsolved murder matched the dates. 29-year-old Japanese student Kayo Matsuzawa was found locked inside a fire alarm cabinet near to where Grimson was teaching, 11 days after she disappeared.

Though a different victim profile and not part of the date theory, the murder was linked to Grimson. It was suspected Kayo was drugged, stripped, and left naked in the airtight cabinet where she suffocated to death. The building manager, who was friendly with Grimson, had seen him in the building on the date of Kayo's disappearance.

A dark stain

Grimson has long since denied connections with other murders or the date theory but investigators still believe he may be responsible for up to 20 murders in total. When some of his interviews were made public, it emerged that Grimson fitted the profile of a thrill killer.

In one interview, he said he used the fire-instructor course to select his victims, from the ranks of trainees and cadets. He would zone-in on the one he enjoyed looking at the most and pass them through to the next stage of training quicker than the rest.

The higher level training was more personal and he was able to dominate and select the best looking trainees for his own pleasure. Then he would scour the local nightclubs looking for them or other men to satisfy his sexual desire.

In 2019, Grimson became eligible for parole and was transferred to an open prison. In Britain, an open prison is a jail in which prisoners are trusted to complete their sentences with minimal supervision. It is generally for prisoners who are considered low-risk to gradually help them reintegrate into society.

For the families of the victims, missing and dead, Grimson's transfer to an open prison was a hammer blow, made worse by the fact the state considered him to be low risk. Whether a serial killer or not, Grimson left a dark stain on the British Navy, one that continues to haunt to this day.

Murder By The Canal

When an abused woman reported her partner to police for assault, she never expected to become instrumental in solving the murder of a young girl twenty years earlier.

In April 2001, while sitting in the waiting room of a courthouse in Winchester, Hampshire, Michelle Jasinskyj nervously awaited the moment she would be called up to testify against her husband, in a domestic violence case that had left her with broken ribs.

Michelle had married Tony Jasinskyj, nine years her senior, in 1988, and went on to have six children with him as the years passed. Soon after their marriage, Tony changed and became violent and aggressive towards her, accusing her of cheating, and controlling her every move.

Tony was an army chef and had been based at the Aldershot army barracks before leaving and taking on a job as a security guard. He attended the Desford Free Church and maintained the image that he had a perfect family life.

In early April 2001, while washing the dishes one night, Michelle found the courage to tell Tony she was leaving him. Asserting his violent control, he came up behind her and punched her in the side of the head, knocking her to the ground.

As she fell, he continued his barrage of punches and kicks and shouting at her all the curse words under the sun. After Tony retreated to the lounge, and despite having broken ribs, Michelle crawled to a neighbour's house where the police were called.

Tony was charged with assault, and a routine DNA swab was taken. A few days later, while waiting to testify against him, Michelle was sitting in the court waiting room, nervous about facing her abuser again, and worried what the future might hold.

A police officer entered the room and Michelle thought the time to testify had come – but the officer had news that was going to change her life forever. Tony's DNA had been run through the database and he had been arrested on suspicion of the rape and murder of a 14-year-old girl, 20 years earlier in 1981.

Canal murder

On Saturday 6th June 1981, 14-year-old Marion Crofts left her home in Basingbourne, Hampshire, to ride her bike to band practice at Wavell School, North Camp, five miles away. It was a route she had taken many times before, and her parents, Trevor and Anne, were confident in her own cycling ability and safety.

Marion was the youngest of three daughters and played clarinet in the band. Most Saturdays, Trevor would drive her to the school but on that fateful day he was due to play in a cricket match at around the same time.

The route took Marion along a part of the Basingstoke Canal, on Laffans Road in Aldershot. Between 9.30am and 10am, she was pushed off her bike and dragged into a small, wooded area beside the road, where she was beaten unconscious.

As she lay dying, the attacker raped her then brutally beat her around the head until she appeared to be dead. A later medical examiner's report concluded she had died from bleeding on the brain caused by massive head injuries.

Her broken body was discovered by a police dog handler later the same day. Her bike and clarinet had been thrown into the Basingstoke Canal and were later recovered by specialist divers. Despite DNA testing in its infancy, forensics collected semen from inside and outside Marion's body.

There were also traces of semen found on her jeans. It was the collection and storage of evidence that would ultimately lead to the capture of Tony Jasinskyj. The material was stored in the belief that technology would advance to such a point that the killer could be found.

The case went cold

In the days following the murder, which shocked the area, the police compiled a list of thousands of suspects, including Tony, but due to a lack of evidence at the time, no one was charged.

The murder of Marion Crofts went cold and ended up on a list of cold case investigations that would only reopen once new leads came in. Though they were not closed cases, they only saw movement if police received a tip or new evidence.

However, due to the police having the forensic material, they planned to input the data into the police database once a year, every year, until the killer was identified. Because of the brutality of the murder, the case didn't stray far from the minds of the investigators involved in it.

In the weeks and months following the murder, Tony began to believe he would get away with it. At the time of the incident, he was based with the Army Catering Corps in Aldershot, only a mile from the murder scene.

Almost all of the military personnel on the base were added to the suspect list but were later removed due to not enough physical or circumstantial evidence. Tony was interviewed and questioned by police about his whereabouts the time of the murder but lied his way out of it

Due to the amount of suspects, the work required to physically check each of them was overbearing and many were crossed off as a matter of routine.

Tony was married at the time and his first wife had no idea what he had done. He divorced her in 1984 and discharged himself from the army. He moved to Leicester, became a security guard, and married Michelle, hoping to escape the horror he had committed on the Crofts family – but the past never forgot.

20 years later

It was Tony's penchant for violence and desire to control others that would ultimately lead to his downfall. When Michelle had gone to the police, she would have had no idea that in some way, she would become responsible for catching a killer.

In 1999, two years before Michelle pressed charges against Tony, police had managed to create a DNA profile based on the forensic material collected from the murder scene. The forensic material had been kept sealed until such time that DNA technology had caught up, so there was no possibility of cross-contamination.

They checked the DNA against the National DNA Database on a regular basis until they got the hit they were waiting for. They discovered that Tony had been arrested for domestic violence and assault and that a routine DNA swab had been taken, leading to the match on the database.

There was no disputing it, Marion's rapist and killer had finally been found, 20 years later. Tony denied the charges and was sent to trial where he pleaded not guilty to rape and murder.

The prosecution proved that the DNA lifted from Marion's body was a one-in-a-billion match for Tony. In 2002, he was sentenced to life for murder and an additional ten years for rape, despite his defence claiming the evidence was flawed.

Justice for all

Justice finally came for the Crofts family, 21 years after Marion's murder. Though their suffering and pain wouldn't entirely come to an end, they would all sleep better knowing that her killer was finally behind bars.

In 2014, Tony and his defence team launched an appeal on the basis that the original trial was flawed because the DNA suggested the killer had a chromosome disorder, which he didn't have. Unsurprisingly, the appeal for wrongful conviction failed.

For Michelle, who lived for years in fear of the violence from her husband, she too could sleep better knowing he was behind bars. But the horror of finding out her husband was a rapist and murderer would never go away.

When her children began asking if they shared the blood of a murderer, she told them to be masters of their own destinies and step away from the shadow of their father. Michelle sat next to Marion's parents when the verdict was read out and they all cheered at the outcome.

If it wasn't for the bravery of one woman standing up to her abuser and reporting him to police, then perhaps Marion's murder would have never been solved and her killer would have never been caught.

The House of Blood Murders

An argument between lovers resulted in a triple murder at a house in Glasgow, branded the House of Blood killings, with the ringleader known as the mother of all evil.

Until 2005, Glasgow, Scotland, was known as the murder capital of Europe, and not without warrant, the city had seen its fair share of horrific deaths. For a while, you were three times more likely to be murdered in Scotland than in England and Wales.

Scotland itself had the second highest European murder rate per capita, ranking close behind Finland, with both countries having a similar population level of 5.5million. To achieve the dishonourable title, Glasgow was witness to an average of 70 murders each year leading up to 2005.

By 2020-2021, murder in Glasgow had fallen by 50% and in that same statistic year had the lowest murder rate since 1976. Nowadays, it is improving, but at the tail end of its reign as Europe's murder capital, a bloody triple murder shocked the city and country.

It became known as the House of Blood killings, one of the bloodiest solved murders in Scotland in the 21st Century. The perpetrators used axes, knives, a hammer, golf clubs, a baseball bat, metal tools, lumps of wood, and a belt, to kill their victims.

And it all began after a lovers argument went wrong – very wrong.

Alcohol changes everything

In the autumn of 2004, 37-year-old Edith McAlinden was released from prison after serving a nine-month sentence for a serious assault. She had previously been convicted for robbery, was known to be a sex worker, and spent a lot of time homeless on the streets of Glasgow.

A few days after being released, on 16th October 2004, Edith went out drinking with her boyfriend, 42-year-old David Gillespie. By the time the evening came around, they had consumed a large amount of alcohol.

While out on the town, they met 67-year-old retired joiner Ian Mitchell, who they were both familiar with. After a few more drinks and getting friendly with them in the pub, Mitchell invited them back to his top floor flat in Crosshill.

Mitchell rented out one of the rooms in the flat to his friend, 71-year-old retired labourer Tony Coyle, who had gone out for the night. Coyle was born in the village of Bloody Foreland in Donegal, Ireland, and was a devout Catholic. Since retirement, he had spent his spare time carrying out repairs and gardening work for elderly neighbours and nearby residents.

Coyle was teetotal and hadn't drunk alcohol since he had retired, while Mitchell enjoyed the occasional drink. Gillespie on the other hand was known to drink heavily and was mostly spurred on by Edith, who always seemed to find a way to get drunk, despite not working.

On that fateful night in October, Edith and Gillespie were drinking heavily in Mitchell's flat when they began arguing with each other. Very quickly, the argument turned violent and Edith began hitting Gillespie.

Then out of nowhere, she grabbed a knife from the kitchen and stabbed him in the thigh. She had unknowingly severed a femoral vein in the leg which meant that Gillespie bled to death on the floor of Mitchell's apartment.

A family affair

Panicked by the thought of going back to prison, Edith refused to phone an ambulance, despite

Mitchell begging her to. Instead, she made a phone call to her son, John, for help. Within minutes, 17-year-old John and his friend, 16-year-old Jamie Gray arrived in a taxi.

Edith begged Mitchell to pay for the taxi, which he did, without informing the taxi driver what had happened. Unbeknownst to Mitchell, Edith hadn't phoned her son for help, she had phoned him to help her eliminate any witnesses to the murder.

Understanding what was happening, John used a different knife and stabbed Mitchell before repeatedly kicking him in the head, causing his brain to bleed. They were wounds that ultimately killed him but they were not finished with him yet.

Shortly after midnight, Coyle returned home from visiting friends and saw that Mitchell's light was on. He popped his head around the door to wish him good night and saw the bloody carnage laid out in front of him.

He ran to his room and locked the door, barricading it with everything he could. Both John and Jamie tried to break the door down, before using drills to take it off the hinges. Once in the room, Jamie beat Coyle to death with a golf club.

But it didn't end there. To ensure the trio were dead, the killers used a wide variety of different weapons to bludgeon and beat their victims. In doing so, blood splattered the walls, sideboards, doors, kitchen units, hallway entrance, and floor.

They also boiled full kettles of water and poured them over Coyle's and Mitchell's heads to see if they were dead. They had killed all the witnesses but now needed to get away with it.

House of blood

Two hours later, at around 3am, without attempting to clean the crime scene, Edith went to a neighbour's house, the home of James Sweeney. She nervously claimed that something terrible had happened at Mitchell's flat and didn't know what to do.

Sweeney entered the flat, and only had to see the bloodied walls of the hallway to know that something horrific had gone down. Without realising there were three victims, he called the emergency services who arrived within minutes.

When police and paramedics arrived, they found Edith in the flat alone, hugging Gillespie's body. She was heard screaming at him to wake up and initially it was suspected the three dead were victims of gang violence, their bodies battered and beaten beyond recognition.

When reporters spoke to Sweeney, he told them of the blood-covered walls and floors, and they ran the story under the headline; *House of Blood*. As the morning hours brought with it a crisp breeze and grey skies, the truth of what happened was still unknown.

Police suggested that due to the amount of blood in the flat and the way it had been spread everywhere, there must have been at least two or three strong men involved. The same day, because of her lack of a cohesive story of what had gone down, Edith was charged with murder.

Mother of all evil

A large investigation began with police still sure that others had been involved. Edith claimed her innocence saying she had gone to the flat to meet her boyfriend and walked into the house of blood.

The investigation also hit an early difficulty, because due to the amount of blood splatter, it became difficult to ascertain the exact details of the violence. The medical examiner's office had on their hands not one, but three of the most brutal deaths they'd seen, and they had their work cut out.

The investigation suspected that Edith had not committed the murders alone and began a manhunt to snare the other culprits but they didn't have to wait long. The forensic team discovered evidence showing that both John and Jamie were involved.

They were arrested the following day and both charged with the murders but the police were not sure who had killed who. In the days that followed, the press got hold of the fact that Edith had called her son to help, which led to the headline; *Mother of all Evil.*

All three went to trial at Glasgow High Court in May 2005 and had initially pleaded not guilty. But as the trial went on, each of them confessed to one murder. Edith to killing Gillespie, John to killing Mitchell, and Jamie to killing Coyle.

Jurors were shown a police video of the murder scene and were warned that it was distressing. The flat had been trashed and covered with broken items and empty bottles of booze. There were also reported to be pieces of skull and brain stuck to the floor and curtains.

One month later, in a very public trial, Edith was convicted of murder and sentenced to life imprisonment with no eligibility for parole until 13 years later in 2018. John and Jamie were convicted of murder and sentenced to a minimum term of 12 years each.

Whereabouts unknown

The sentences were deemed to be too lenient by family members of the victims and they erupted in anger when the sentences were read out in court. A campaign was created to get the sentences extended but it ultimately went nowhere.

In early 2016, John was released a year early, but in November 2018 found himself back behind bars after threatening and abusing his girlfriend on a Glasgow street. His girlfriend refused to testify against him but John went back to jail for breaching the terms of his release.

Jamie was released early too but his whereabouts are unknown. Though he was 16 at the time, he was still considered an adult, and it is assumed he changed his identity to move on with a new life.

As for Edith, she initially had a tough time of it in prison, as fellow female prisoners were out for her blood, in revenge for the brutality of her crimes. She avoided being attacked by changing her demeanour and embarking on lesbian relationships with many other prisoners.

Details of her 'sex romps' and prison violence were given to the press when one of her lovers was released from her sentence for drug dealing. It further cemented Edith's reputation as one of Glasgow's, and Scotland's, worst female criminals.

A search of the prison system showed that Edith had completed her sentence in 2018 and was released in 2019. Her whereabouts remain unknown and her identity hidden, most likely for her own protection.

Few in Crosshill or Glasgow will ever forget the brutality that Edith McAlinden inflicted on their city in 2004. Even under the unfortunate statistic of the murder capital of Europe, the House of Blood is a tale of triple murder that's hard to wash away.

The Oxford Student Murder

A football fan watched his team win the FA Cup semi-final, then killed his girlfriend, hid the corpse under the floorboards of her house, and weaved an elaborate tale in an attempt to outwit the police.

O xford is not usually the place one might associate with murder, but in 1991, the murder of 19-year-old St. Hilda's College student, Rachel McLean, hit the headlines. At first, it was a mysterious disappearance but as time went on, police concluded she had been killed.

Born in 1971, Rachel was a second-year student studying English Language and was on the road to success, backed up by wealthy parents and an even better academic profile. She was the eldest of three children with two younger brothers.

Her mother, Joan, was head of foreign language at a school in Poulton-le-Fylde, a town close to Blackpool where Rachel was born. Her father, Malcolm, was an engineer for British Aerospace with a high wage and higher respect among his peers.

Rachel met her future boyfriend, John Tanner, when he worked over the Summer in the Adam and Eve nightclub in Oxford. She invited him to her 19th birthday at her family home in Carleton, near Blackpool, and they hit it off.

Tanner was three years her senior, a 22-year-old student at the University of Nottingham studying Greek and Roman Classic Literature and History. He was born in Hampshire but emigrated to New Zealand with his parents when he was just a few months old.

He moved back to England when he was 17, and after a three year stint in New Zealand in 1989, returned to study in Nottingham. As such, he had dual citizenship status for both countries. He was a popular student around campus and was the elected student union representative for one of the halls of residence.

While at the University, he hosted a twice-weekly talk show called The Fast Lane and played football on Saturdays. No one could have suspected at the time that Tanner would go on to commit murder.

Restricted by his presence

While in Oxford, Rachel was elected vice-president of her college junior common room and became a member of the Oxford Union and Industrial Society. Rachel and Tanner had a good relationship to a point and wrote each other letters when they were apart.

It was the distance between them that became a problem for Tanner. They studied 100 miles apart, and as Tanner couldn't see Rachel as often as he would have liked, he began to feel threatened by her and became obsessed with controlling every little detail of her life from afar.

Rachel began to feel restricted by his presence, and his obsession had become unbearable. Despite Tanner claiming they were so in love and had sex up to seven times a day, Rachel's diary revealed a different story.

She wrote that she had grown to despise her boyfriend and pointed to his obsession with keeping her close as one of the major factors. She found him childish, and one line in her diary read; *'you are so busy generating self-pity that you cannot see how you slice me to pieces.'* It was perhaps an unfortunate omen of what was to come.

Rachel lived in a ground floor room in a house on Argyle Street, Oxford, that she shared with four other students. On Saturday 13th April, at the tail-end of the Easter break, Rachel spent the day with her mother, who left at 4pm to drive back home to Blackpool.

Tanner was due to arrive at Oxford on the train at 6pm and Rachel had gone to meet him at the station. Due to delays on the service, the arrival time was changed to 7pm. Not wanting to hang around on a fresh spring evening, Rachel went back to her house, and room.

At 7.30pm, Tanner arrived at the house and they spent the night together alone, as none of the other students had returned from Easter break. That night, Tanner proposed to Rachel but she said she needed to sleep on it and would give him the answer the next day.

Beneath the floorboards

The following day, on Sunday the 14th, Tanner was eager to watch his team, Nottingham Forest, play in the FA Cup semi-final against West Ham, that afternoon. He sat in the shared lounge of the house watching the game, as Rachel studied on the computer in her room.

Despite his team winning 4-0 and progressing to the finals, Tanner wasn't happy, as he still hadn't received a response to his proposal. At around 4.30pm, a neighbour saw the pair arguing loudly outside the house.

Rachel was telling Tanner that she didn't want to be engaged to him due to his possessiveness and controlling behaviour. The neighbour was the second-to-last person to see Rachel alive. The last person to see her alive was Tanner, as he strangled the life from her.

At some point that evening, Tanner snapped and put both hands around Rachel's neck. He squeezed until she fell unconscious then tied a ligature around her neck to ensure she was dead. He put her body on the bed and spent the night on the floor beside it. When the morning of Monday the 15th came around, and the other students hadn't yet returned to the house, he spent several hours looking for a hiding place for the body. He decided the cupboard under the stairs was the best place to hide her.

He emptied the junk that was in there and dragged Rachel's body from her room next door. At the back of the cupboard there was a small gap, only eight-inches across, covered with junk that led to the space underneath the floorboards.

He pushed her body into the gap then climbed in himself and crawled under the hallway, dragging her body to a location that was under the floorboards of her own room. He then filled the cupboard back up with the junk and put together an elaborate plan to get himself off the hook.

A fake paper trail

Tanner left the house later that afternoon and took the bus to Oxford station to catch the

6.30pm train back to Nottingham. While on the train, he wrote a love letter to Rachel saying how much they were meant to be together.

In the letter, he posited that Rachel had gone with him to the station and that she was driven back to the house by an unidentified male friend. He wrote; *'Fancy seeing that friend of yours at the station. It was nice of him to give you a lift. But I hate him because he has longer hair than me. Ha ha!'*

On Tuesday the 16th, Tanner posted the letter then phoned Rachel's house to show that he was curious as to her whereabouts. Unsurprisingly, there was no answer. For the first couple of days at least, no one had any idea that something horrific had gone down.

On Wednesday evening, he phoned again, and 20-year-old student Victoria Clare answered, who was one of the other students living in the house. Tanner spoke in a positive manner and asked to talk to Rachel but Victoria confirmed she wasn't in the house. It also wasn't abnormal for a student to take extra time off, and even in some shared houses, some students kept themselves to themselves.

Tanner's letter arrived on Thursday the 18th, and he phoned the house again but of course Rachel was nowhere to be seen. On Friday the 19th, her housemates became concerned as she was due to attend an important meeting with her tutor that morning but didn't show.

One of the students in the house phoned Rachel's mother, Joan, to find out when Rachel was last seen, and Joan confirmed that she had been in Oxford the previous weekend. Tanner confirmed to Rachel's parents and her housemates that he had left on the Monday morning. His letter and phone calls initially backed him up – but the investigation was about to begin.

No evidence and no body

After Rachel failed to show at the college, her friends and the college authorities called the police and reported her as missing. Because Oxford has a large student population, police often received calls of missing students who inevitably turned up later for various reasons, and they weren't always top of the list for incidents to investigate.

A week after her disappearance, Oxford detectives took over the case and got a warrant to look at Rachel's room. They carried out an extensive search of the room but concluded that the floorboards had not been tampered with.

On Monday 22nd, after her disappearance became public knowledge, detectives confirmed there was no evidence of any wrongdoing in her room. They contacted Tanner by phone who told them he had last seen Rachel at Oxford train station a week earlier.

To put police off the scent, Tanner reiterated the fact that there was a long-haired man at the station who knew Rachel and offered to give her a lift home. At the same time, police found his letter, and it seemed to back up the fact that the mysterious long-haired man was the last person to see Rachel alive.

Despite the suggestion of the mystery man, detectives were already suspicious of Tanner, for a number of reasons. Rachel didn't have any male friends who had long hair, and a witness statement from the neighbour proved they had argued before she disappeared.

There was also Rachel's diary that showed Tanner had controlling tendencies and that she was on the verge of splitting up with him, which pointed to a possible motive. Though they suspected him of being responsible for her disappearance and possible murder, they had no evidence – and no body.

Prime suspect

Police decided to use a press conference as part of their own investigation. On Wednesday 24th April, Tanner and Rachel's parents went on national TV and appealed for help in finding Rachel. However, the journalists were given specific questions by police they could ask, without stating outright that Tanner was their suspect.

They wanted to see his reactions to some of the questions. Tanner was sandwiched between two detectives, away from Rachel's parents, who had no idea Tanner was a suspect. One reporter suggested Tanner give a message to anyone holding Rachel against her will.

He said, '*I would appeal to them to come forward and tell us, just out of sheer consideration for her mother and father and myself.*' When asked if he had killed her, he answered with a smirk, '*I did not kill her.*' Then asked if he thought she was still alive, '*in my heart of hearts I would like to think so.*'

Though it didn't entirely prove Tanner was the killer, detectives involved in the case put him down as their prime suspect, based on his lack of emotion. Working on the basis she had been murdered, police search teams scoured nearby marshland, local sewers, and septic tanks, then dragged the waters of the nearby River Cherwell.

Tanner then agreed to take part in a reconstruction of their last moments together, including his supposed final kiss at the train station. As a result of it, witnesses came forward to say they had seen Tanner at the station but that he was alone. No one, it seemed, could place Rachel at the station.

Realising she had disappeared between the house and the station, police checked the original plans of the houses in Argyle Street, hoping to find closed-off basements, which they didn't. They discovered the house had been underpinned in their original construction, which meant there were larger than normal gaps beneath the floorboards.

They obtained a warrant for the entire house, and on 2nd May, as the sun was going down, they discovered Rachel's body, 18 days after she had been killed.

A well-practiced façade

Tanner was arrested as he drank in a pub in Nottingham and initially refused to say anything. In his second interview with police, and on advice from his lawyer, he claimed that he did kill Rachel but that it had been an accident and denied the act of murder.

At his trial, Tanner still tried to play games with the authorities by claiming that it had been Rachel's fault. He had become angry at her after she had allegedly mocked him for being unable to perform sexually, despite him telling friends that he had sex up to seven times a night.

Fortunately, due to the cold spring weather and the fact that Tanner had covered Rachel's body with carpet, there was minimal decomposition, which meant a coroner could ascertain the cause of death as manual strangulation.

It could have been accidental until they realised a ligature had been used after to ensure she was dead. Tanner had not tried to resuscitate her or thought about calling an ambulance, as he had been more concerned with saving himself.

On 6th December 1991, he was convicted of murder and sentenced to life in prison. In 2003, after serving a little over 11 years, he was released on good behaviour and immediately moved back to New Zealand, despite the minimum life term set at 15 years.

But maybe Tanner's 'good behaviour' was a well-practiced façade, because in 2018, Tanner was jailed for three years for attacking his new girlfriend in New Zealand. He had abused her over a six-month period and forced her to have sex with him multiple times.

On one occasion there had been a ghastly reminder of the past when Tanner had put his hands around her neck and restricted her breathing. Fortunately, history didn't repeat itself then, but Tanner was released in 2021 and his whereabouts are unknown.

The Ughill Hall Murders

In a double murder that shocked Sheffield, a successful solicitor killed his mistress and her daughter, and left her son for dead, before fleeing to France and threatening to jump off the Amiens Cathedral.

With an urban population of 730,000 (2020), Sheffield is one of the largest cities in the UK and played a big part historically in the Industrial Revolution from 1760 to 1840. It also has a long sporting history and is home to Sandygate; the world's oldest football ground, first opened in 1804.

History plays a big part in the city and so it's no surprise that crime has also left its mark. Now considered a relatively safe city, Sheffield has been home to some of the most notorious murders in middle England, including The East House Murders and The Blonk Street Murder.

But there is one incident from the 1980s that seemed to have a bigger effect on locals, with many claiming to have links to the family involved, and the survivor of the attack. It forever tainted the quaint village of Ughill, on the outskirts of the city.

On 21st September 1986, solicitor Ian Wood shot dead his French mistress, Danielle Ledez, her three-year-old daughter Stephanie, and left her five-year-old son Christopher for dead, after shooting him twice in the head.

He fled to France and went on the run before climbing the Cathedral Basilica of Our Lady of Amiens, also known as the Amiens Cathedral, in the Picardy region of the country, and threatening to jump to his death in front of a large crowd.

Splashing the cash

The whole sordid affair began a few years earlier when Wood left his wife of a number of years and his three children to hook up with his French mistress, Danielle. Wood, born in 1949, was a successful solicitor, and the fruits of his labour were large.

So large in fact, that in 1986 at the age of 37, he was able to rent an 18-bedroom mansion called Ughill Hall. Within the confines of Sheffield, he had set up his own legal practice with many employees and had become chairman of the Sheffield Law Society.

Known as a bit of a playboy, he was open to splashing the cash while out and about, regularly hosted dinner parties for some of Sheffield's finest, and was known to buy lavish gifts for others, either to keep them close or as a display of wealth.

He began renting Ughill Hall in April 1986 and moved in with Danielle and her two children. Danielle was a French teacher from Amiens, who was living in England when she met Wood.

She was in the process of divorcing her second husband when she moved into Ughill Hall, and was already 10 weeks pregnant, allegedly with Wood's child, though the unborn child's parentage was never proven.

Gun collector turned murderer

Wood was a gun collector, who had inherited a .38 Enfield revolver from his father after he took his own life with it. The gun was the standard British sidearm used during the Second World War and was manufactured between 1930 and 1957.

His father's suicide left an indelible mark on Wood's life and was something he would later use in his defence at the trial. By 1985, Wood had amassed a collection of 10 guns that were stored at his home, where he lived with his first wife.

In December 1985, when he turned to alcohol because of existing mental health conditions, including depression, his wife had the collection officially confiscated. The collection was returned to Wood two weeks later as South Yorkshire Police couldn't find any evidence to suggest he was a threat to himself or others, despite being diagnosed with depression.

A few weeks after that, the guns were confiscated again due to an administrative mix-up with his firearm license. They were returned a second time in February 1986. A month later in March, Wood purchased 50 rounds of ammunition for his father's revolver.

On the night of 21st September 1986, and for reasons then unknown, Wood, then 37, decided to kill his new family. At around midnight, he went to the playroom of the mansion where Danielle was resting and murdered her with a bullet to the head.

He then took three-year-old Stephanie from her bedroom and asked her to play hide and seek. She sleepily agreed and he led her to Christopher's bedroom, where he shot her twice in the back of the head, killing her instantly. Five-year-old Christopher was removed from his bedroom and taken to one of the bathrooms.

Wood told him to close his eyes as he had a surprise for him. When Christopher put his hands over his eyes, Wood shot him twice in the head at point blank range, then used a large metal ruler to beat him before leaving his body with the others in the playroom. Remarkably, Christopher would go on to survive the attack.

Miracle survivor

Wood then calmly began the process of leaving the mansion. He packed a suitcase, changed his clothes, and left the property in the early hours of the morning. He left the revolver on the kitchen worktop, with one live round inside.

He drove to Dover in a rented car and caught a ferry to France later that morning. Shortly before he boarded, he phoned the police and told them he had murdered Danielle and her family. On the evening of the 22nd, police arrived at the mansion.

All the doors and windows were locked, and with no answer, they smashed down the front door. Due to the size of the mansion, they didn't find the bodies immediately, but when they entered the playroom, they walked in on a grizzly sight.

The two children had been laid next to their mother in a pool of blood. It was clear to police they had all been shot, but when one officer checked Christopher's body for signs of life, he was shocked to discover the boy was alive.

After 21 hours of laying on the floor next to his family members, Christopher was rushed to Royal

Hallamshire Hospital for children where doctors fought to save his life. Two bullets were removed from his head, and he was placed on life support.

On the run

Believing Wood to still be in and around Sheffield, police put his wife and three children under police protection and warned the public not to approach him as he may have been in possession of a firearm. Four additional families were placed under police protection in relation to the case.

Two days after the murders, on the 23rd, Wood phoned a reporter called Brenda Tunny who worked for the local Sheffield Weekly Gazette. She interrupted a police press conference to inform them of the contact she'd had.

During the phone call, Wood had asked about funeral arrangements and told her how he killed the family. Over the next few days, he phoned Brenda another eight times. Over the course of the phone calls, he spoke about taking his own life, and claimed he killed Danielle due to a suicide pact but refused to give his location.

Shortly after the first phone call, an AA (Automobile Association) admin clerk contacted police and told them Wood had applied for an international driving license. Interpol were called in, and the investigation linked up with French authorities.

On 29th September, eight days after the murders, and with international attention focused on the case, Wood travelled to Amiens where he joined a public tour of Amiens Cathedral. The famous building was only three miles from where Danielle had been born.

He left the tour group and climbed to the top of the cathedral where he stepped over the top wall and roped himself to a gargoyle. The intention was to jump off the gargoyle to hang himself, 61-metres (200ft) from the hard ground below.

The authorities arrived quickly after receiving multiple reports and discovered that Wood had left a suicide note with a member of staff. He remained roped to the gargoyle for almost seven hours until a local priest, assisted by the police, talked him down.

Suicide pact

Wood was taken into custody and claimed that when he saw the amount of people gathered on the ground watching him, he couldn't jump as he didn't want an audience for his death. After a lengthy extradition process, Wood was flown back to the UK on 19th November to face trial.

The trial began in early February 1987 and Wood was charged with two counts of murder and one of attempted murder. He pleaded guilty to Stephanie's murder and Christopher's attempted murder but pleaded not guilty to Danielle's murder. He claimed that it was manslaughter and not murder, because they had agreed to a suicide pact.

In the UK at the time, there was a law that stated if a person killed another person on the basis of a suicide pact and didn't take their own life after, then they would be guilty of manslaughter and not murder – but they needed to prove there was a pact in place.

Wood's defence put forward his five step suicide pact. Wood was to kill the family then visit a French church to light candles for them. Then phone the press and explain what had happened, kill Danielle's husband, ensure they were all buried in France, then visit their graves and lay flowers for them.

The unusual five step pact was not believed and Wood was found guilty of two murders and one attempted murder. In July 1987, Wood was sentenced to life imprisonment for each murder and an additional 12 years for attempted murder.

After the trial, the police were scrutinised for allowing Wood to have access to so many weapons. Wood's doctor had advised the police to confiscate the weapons just weeks before the murders, on the basis that Wood appeared mentally distressed.

Life finds a way

Less than a month later, on 19th August, 27-year-old Michael Ryan shot dead 16 people in Berkshire, in an event that became known as the Hungerford Massacre. Both events saw the government pass the Firearms Act 1988 which banned ownership of semi-automatic weapons and required psychiatric assessments to be completed.

The courthouse where the trial took place was abandoned in 1997 and left to rot, becoming a popular site for urban explorers. In 2019, plans had been submitted by new owners to turn it into a hotel but failed when they ran into financial trouble. The giant building went to auction in 2021 at a guide price of only £750,000 but got no bidders. It remains abandoned.

Wood's whereabouts are unknown but he was suspected to have been moved to a locked psychiatric facility, and as such, is difficult to track. If he had been released, it would have happened quietly and under a new name.

Christopher Ledez made a recovery but was physically and mentally scarred by the shootings. He has never publicly spoken about what happened but is known to have moved on with his life, is now married, and has children of his own, proving that life will always find a way.

The Case of the Green Bicycle Murder

A murder mystery involving a female victim, bloody bird prints, a dead crow, a gun in a canal, a pea-green bicycle, and a 100-year search for the truth, in a case fit for Sherlock Holmes.

In a murder mystery worthy of an Agatha Christie novel, the unsolved case of the green bicycle captivated the nation and has continued to be written and spoken about a hundred years later, with many researchers putting forward their theories.

On 5th July 1919, 21-year-old Bella Wright was shot in the face and died of her wound immediately. She was found later that evening next to her bicycle. For months, the case made no progress until a bargeman discovered the frame of a green bicycle in a canal.

Bella was born in 1897 and was the eldest of seven children to a farmer and his wife. From the age of 17, she worked at a rubber factory in Leicester, just five miles from her home in Stoughton, where she'd lived all her life in a quaint thatched cottage with her large family.

Her cheeriness was infectious, and her love for life was admirable, and as such she became popular with the local boys, but she wanted a higher class of man. She met a Royal Navy engineer named Archie Ward, who worked on the HMS Diadem, a training ship based in Portsmouth.

They were engaged to be married but Bella was unsure if she would go through with it, and according to her mother, had fallen in love with another officer in the Royal Navy. There was local suspicion she was seeing someone else at the same time but the name remains lost to the annals of history.

Bella regularly cycled from her home to the factory and took the same route on most days, along the scenic Grand Union Canal in Leicester. It was on a lonely country lane near to the canal where her dead body was to be discovered.

A bloody crow

Alongside cycling to work, she also rode around the local villages, running errands, meeting friends, and picking up goods from shops. After one of the coldest winters on records, the warm summer of 1919 was most welcome and the cycling industry was starting to really take off.

On that fateful evening, Bella was cycling from her uncle's house near to the village of Little Stretton when she was killed by a bullet to the face. When the body was reported to police half hour later, they assumed she had died in an unfortunate accident.

In the dark of night, they moved the body to a nearby cottage while another officer went back to the scene. On the ground were bloody bird prints that led away from where Bella's body had been to the top of a nearby wooden gate. Beyond the gate in the meadow, a crow with bloody feet lay dead.

The long grass of the meadow had been recently flattened into a makeshift footpath that led away to the cornfields in the distance. Suspecting something untoward had gone down, the officer returned to Bella's body, wiped the blood from her face, and found a bullet hole below her left eye.

It appeared her death was no accident and they were dealing with a mysterious case of murder. The next day, the same officer returned to the lane and found a bullet pressed into the ground by a horseshoe. An autopsy revealed the bullet had passed through Bella's face and out through the back of her head, staining her straw hat with blood.

Mystery green bicycle

Within hours, witnesses came forward to claim they had seen Bella riding her bike next to a scruffy-looking man on a pea-green bicycle. They couldn't identify him but said he had been wearing a grey suit, grey cap, shirt and tie, and black boots.

Her uncle said she had left his house with a man on a green bike who she referred to by name but he couldn't remember what she had said. If the murder had taken place in today's world, forensics would have scoured the region en-masse, but 100 years ago, it was a different story.

All the police had to go on was the sighting of the man on the green bicycle, a dead crow, and crushed grass leading away from the scene. Six days later, as the police were still investigating the murder, Bella was buried at a funeral attended by hundreds of locals.

Soon after, the case went cold and Bella's death passed over into the unsolved – until seven months later. On a cold morning in February 1920, a barge on the River Soar snagged itself on an object on the riverbed, which turned out to be the frame of a pea-green bicycle.

Suddenly, police had what could have been a vital piece of evidence and reopened the Bella case file. Most of the serial numbers had been filed off but an expert reconstructed the number and tracked it to a bike shop owner in Derby who had sold it to 34-year-old maths teacher Ronald Vivian Light, nine years earlier.

Born in 1885, Light had a troubled childhood despite coming from a wealthy family. He was the son of a wealthy civil engineer who managed a coal mine. Light was expelled from Oakham School in 1902, aged 17, when he lifted a young girl's clothes over her head. He also admitted to sexual contact with a 15-year-old and was caught acting suspiciously around an eight-year-old.

A broken man

He went on to graduate as a civil engineer from the University of Birmingham, aged 21, and became employed as an architect and draughtsman at Midland Railway. He was fired from the job in 1914 when he was suspected of causing a fire and writing lewd comments in the toilets.

Light was also known to have forged military orders during his brief stint with the army following the outbreak of the First World War. He served for two years and was court-martialled when it was uncovered he had faked his own move orders.

He also deliberately caused a fire at a farm by setting light to the haystacks. None of the previous information was heard by the jury at his subsequent trial, which may have made a difference to the outcome.

While he was in the army, Light's father died by suicide, and upon returning home to live with his mother in early 1919, Light was provided with community psychiatric care. He claimed that the army had sent him home as a broken man.

At first, Light denied owning the green bicycle, then changed his story to say he had sold it to an anonymous buyer while he was in the army. Already suspicious of Light, police dredged the canal near to where Bella had been found. To their surprise, they found a brown leather army-issue gun holster.

There was no gun inside but there were bullets clipped away that matched the same bullet found beside the body. The holster was matched to the one Light was suspected to have smuggled from his army base. The police were then under no illusion that they had caught the suspect.

The trial of Light

The trial began in June 1920 with Light pleading not guilty. He was fortunate to be represented by one of the great barristers of the time, Edward Marshall Hall. The prosecution had a simple story in place as to what they believed happened.

They suggested that Light had been cycling along the same path when he decided to ride alongside

Bella. He attempted to woo her but Bella rejected his advances. In a fit of rage, Light pushed her to the ground then shot her in the face where she fell.

The defence, led by Hall, posited Light's side of the story. Light had been riding beside the canal when he noticed Bella attempting to tighten a loose wheel. She asked him for help but he didn't have the right tools to assist her.

Realising she was headed in the same direction as him, Light offered to ride with her. He waited for her outside her uncle's house much to the bemusement of her uncle, who had asked Bella if she was okay, which she claimed she was. The pair rode off together along the country lane just before 9pm.

When they approached the junction at King's Norton, Bella told him that she was headed off on a different route and they parted ways. Light claimed to have ridden straight home and did not know about the death until three days later when he read about it in the news.

It occurred to Light that he was one of the last people to see Bella alive and it concerned him. Three months later, in October, he removed his bike from the attic, filed off the serial numbers, took it apart, and dumped it in the River Soar.

The prosecution took testimony from the maid of Light's mother, who stated that Light hadn't returned home until 10pm the night of the murder and had destroyed all the clothing he had worn throughout that day.

Two local underage girls also testified and claimed they had been accosted by Light three hours before the murder and that he had pestered them for sexual favours. They were riding their bikes close to the location where Bella was ultimately found.

No logical motive

The trial was being pulled in all different directions and the jury had a tough time on their hands. Hall managed to convince the court that a bullet fired from Light's gun would have caused a much larger wound and suggested the bullet had come from a high-powered rifle instead.

He went as far as stating there hadn't been a murder at all, and that Bella had been shot as a result of an unfortunate accident. She had ridden into the path of a hunter's bullet, by someone out shooting birds, which explained the bloody bird prints near the body and the dead crow.

Light admitted lying to police and agreed with witness statements that he was seen riding with Bella but denied being in possession or having used his army revolver. As with the green bicycle, he had thrown his gun into the river at the same time to avoid suspicion.

The prosecution cross-examined Light for five hours and he never contradicted himself. They also couldn't prove beyond reasonable doubt that he was responsible for Bella's death, as everything he was saying could not be disproved.

Yet, the biggest flaw in the prosecution's case was that they could not present a logical motive, instead hoping the circumstantial evidence would be good enough for a conviction. As such, on 11th June 1920, Light was found not guilty of murder and released as a free man.

Who killed Bella?

On the basis the jury didn't believe Light was the murderer, it suggested that they too had believed the tragic accident angle that Bella was hit by a stray bullet. Light slipped away to a new life after spending a few months with his mother and was known to have died in 1975 at the age of 89 in Kent.

The murder of Bella Wright remains unsolved and continues to fascinate researchers – and cyclists – to this day. In 2019, 100 years later, a 'green bicycle murder ride' took place along the route of the incident with events leading to the death recreated by period actors.

The only reason Light was suspected to be the killer was because of the green bicycle. Without the high-level of record-keeping by the bike shop owner, whose accounts and sales records went back over a decade, Light may never have been a suspect.

Which begs the question – was Bella murdered or was she the victim of an unfortunate accident? As it stands, there is simply not enough evidence to prove it either way. It seems unusual that a crow walked away from the body with bloodied feet, suggesting the crow was close by when Bella was shot.

Maybe Light was showing-off his shooting skills to Bella and tried to shoot a crow for her. When the crow descended a little too fast, he took a shot not realising he had fired in her direction. Perhaps Light deliberately killed her and in the end got away with murder.

Or maybe, an unidentified hunter was in the area and shot a crow at the same time Bella rode in front of it. The hunter may not have ever realised he had killed someone. Despite the theories, the case of the green bicycle murder remains a mystery that continues to divide true crime fans to this day.

The Midlands Ripper

A lorry driver with a hatred of women killed two sex workers in Leicestershire, resulting in Operation Enigma that reviewed the unsolved murders of 200 more.

P upils from the same school referred to Alun Kyte as a sickly youngster. He was known to suffer from severe asthma and always kept an inhaler nearby in case of a sudden attack. Though he didn't have many friends, his mother and two sisters doted on him.

Born in 1964 in the Stoke-on-Trent village of Tittensor, his family moved to the Rickerscote area of Stafford soon after, where he was raised. From a young age, Kyte preferred to be by himself but managed to get through school with mixed grades.

Kyte took on a series of dead-end jobs when he left school but failed to hold them down for any length of time. He was known to live in hostels and guesthouses all over the United Kingdom, claiming that he was looking for work where there was none back home.

He travelled hundreds of miles each week looking for mysterious, elusive jobs, though some later claimed he may have been killing at the same time. Then he landed his dream job as a lorry driver which meant he could move around the country with a perfect alibi.

No one really knew who Kyte was, as he lived a private life, preferring to be alone. He was rarely seen with women and only occasionally frequented the local Stafford pubs where he would be content to play pool and drink with himself.

Little did anyone know at the time that Kyte was a murderer of women and would later be connected to more victims than Peter Sutcliffe; The Yorkshire Ripper. Behind Kyte's soft, reassuring Staffordshire accent, there was a maniac hiding in plain sight.

Hunter killer

Most serial killers are creatures of opportunity and unplanned chaos, they are rarely cunning and rely on fortunate circumstance to commit their crimes. Those like Kyte are different, they are hunters, learning from previous attempts, moving victims between crimes scenes and understanding how to keep the police off their scent.

In-between lorry driving, Kyte ran a fraudulent mobile car tuning service and would delay returning cars to customers by up to three weeks, duping them into paying out more money, despite not having made their cars any better.

Unknown to his customers, he was driving their cars around the country looking for locations where he could select his victims. One vehicle was returned to their owner with an extra 1,000 miles on the clock. Kyte would sometimes stay in paid accommodation under the car owner's name.

When he needed to get more money, he began stealing goods from national DIY stores then returning them with no receipt, requesting refunds. He was also a regular at many hospitals around the country where he would collect prescriptions for his asthma medication.

In early December 1993, in Birmingham's Balsall Heath red light district, Kyte picked up 20-year-old single parent and sex worker Samo Paull. He drove her to a lay-by near junction 20 of the M1 motorway, raped her at knifepoint then strangled her to death.

Her partially-nude body was found three weeks later on 31st December by a horse rider who was riding near to a water-logged ditch. Samo's body was identified by her family but all her possessions had been stolen by her killer which led to the suspicion her boyfriend was involved.

When discovery of her body was made public, a witness came forward with an unusual story.

Driving the dead

The day after Samo went missing, Betty Wilson was driving to work when she noticed a brown Ford Sierra parked on a grassy verge. It was unusual as it was early in the day and the car had its headlights on full beam.

She slowed down to get a closer look and saw the car was covered in mud, which made her suspect the car had come off the road at some point. She saw a man in the driver's seat, who pulled down his hat as she passed by, and couldn't get a good look at his face.

Then Betty noticed a woman in the back seat wearing a black dress with mottled skin and strange marks on her face, her eyes were open and she was sitting deadly still. Unknown to Betty at the time, she was looking at the body of Samo, but didn't stop as she was already late for work.

On 2nd March 1994, a reconstruction of Samo's murder was broadcast on national television. Kyte was watching and he remembered the thrill he got from murdering Samo, which led him to kill another victim that very night.

He picked up 30-year-old Tracey Turner from Hilton Park motorway services on the M6. Tracey was a stocky and partially deaf sex worker who had been paying her way with sex since the age of 15 and made the fateful decision to step into Kyte's car.

At 8am the next day, a teacher was driving to work through the small village of Bitteswell, Leicester, when they noticed something unusual on the side of the road. The teacher reversed the car and discovered Tracey's nude body on her back on a grassy verge.

Tracey had been raped, stripped, and strangled to death. The location of the body was only six miles away from where Samo had been found and was close to the M1, but police made no connection between the two bodies at the time.

A close encounter

A few days earlier, the country had been rocked by the Fred and Rose West House of Horrors story, in which 12 murders had been committed. As such, the newspapers were jam-packed with that story, leaving little room for the murder of prostitutes.

One suspect was a Glaswegian man who was parked at the motorway services at the time. His number plate was tracked to his home but investigators found no evidence to connect him to the murder. Two days after the murder, Kyte brazenly returned to the services and posed as a reporter investigating prostitution in the area.

Though there are many more murders linked to Kyte, none have been conclusively proven. But there are violent attacks that took place in which Kyte was the prime suspect and has been linked to them by police work.

Two weeks after Tracey's murder, a third sex worker had a close encounter with Kyte. On a wet March night in Balsall Heath's red light district, the sex worker was picked up by Kyte who drove her a few miles down the road to the dark car park of the Moseley Hall Hospital.

Kyte then reached for a Stanley knife and put it to her neck, ordering her to hand over her house keys and purse, and to strip for him. She told Kyte that she was three months pregnant and his demeanour changed. At the mention of a baby, Kyte kicked her out of the car and drove off at high speed.

She reported it to police and they tentatively connected the attack to the two murders but no suspect was found. Kyte managed to evade police detection despite being arrested for shoplifting many times in various locations.

Mounting evidence

The two murders went unsolved for almost four years until Kyte attacked again. In December 1997, Kyte was staying at a hostel in Weston-Super-Mare where he raped and sodomised another guest. The victim escaped, fled the hostel and went straight to police.

Kyte was arrested by waiting police officers as he attempted to flee the hostel. At a subsequent trial, he was found guilty of rape and sentenced to eight years in prison, and still he had not been connected to the murders.

Shortly after the sentencing, the police took a routine sample and matched Kyte's DNA to the forensic material found on Tracey's body. DNA profiling was still in its infancy, and though the match should have been made before the rape trial, it was at least made soon after.

He was charged with Tracey's murder in May 1998. After the link had been made to Tracey, it wasn't long before he was positively linked to Samo's murder. Kyte denied being involved and claimed he had never used sex workers but the evidence was mounting against him.

Kyte had boasted of the murders while on remand, was seen on CCTV posing as a reporter at the services, had DNA matches on not just one, but two murder victims, and had been imprisoned for a violent rape. He was convicted in 2000 of both murders and sentenced to a minimum of 25 years in prison.

As more victims were being inconclusively attributed to Kyte, the press referred to him as the Midlands Ripper, suggesting he may have killed more people than the Yorkshire Ripper.

Operation Enigma

By 1996, police in Britain were becoming inundated with murders of sex workers, so much so that Operation Enigma was created to help solve them. The investigation team found 207 murders of prostitutes or those that may have appeared to be sex workers, in the previous ten years, from 1986 to 1996. The job was to solve them.

In the six month period following Samo's murder, four more sex workers, including Tracey, were murdered across the country, leading to a cross-force investigation that resulted in the creation of Britain's first violent crime database.

To this day, most remain unsolved, leading to the suspicion that multiple serial killers had been murdering sex workers throughout the 1980s and 1990s. Most victims had similarities to each other in the locations they were found, method of murder, and linked witness statements.

The Operation Enigma investigation team investigated all 207 and found 72 that needed further analysis. They linked 14 additional murders to Kyte that were of particular interest, which were backed up by later researchers. In prison, Kyte confessed to killing 12 women.

Somewhere along the line, Kyte had developed a hatred of women, especially sex workers he felt were below his standards. In his prison confession to another inmate, he said that he wouldn't pay to have sex with a certain type of woman and that they deserved everything he did to them.

Of the 14 suspected murders, many were in locations where Kyte was known to have been in the vicinity, and all were found close to major motorways. Over the years, investigations have narrowed down the victim list to eight.

Because there was no DNA taken in a lot of the cases, there has never been enough evidence to charge Kyte with them. In August 2013, Kyte's team failed in an appeal to reduce his sentence which meant he would need to serve the minimum of 25 years before release.

On the basis of the links between various cases from Operation Enigma, investigators concluded that at least four more serial killers were active in the UK from 1986 to 1996, with a potential pool of over 50 victims between them. None of the four have yet been identified.

Murder in the Red Barn

A sensational 19th Century murder, an illegitimate child, a supernatural dream, a shallow grave, an evil squire, and a red barn, make for one of the most notorious olde English murder cases.

A nn Marten had not seen her stepdaughter, Maria, in eleven months and was becoming more and more worried with every passing season. Maria had supposedly eloped from the family home in Polstead, Suffolk, on 18th May 1827, to Ipswich, with her lover, local farmer William Corder.

Ann and her molecatcher husband, Thomas, would often write letters to Maria to find out what she was up to and to let her know they loved her. But Maria wouldn't reply, and whenever William returned to Polstead, he would give various excuses as to her absence and failure to respond.

He claimed that the mail must have vanished en-route, she had injured her hand, was busy with work, or that she simply forgot to respond. He assured them that their daughter was beyond happy in Ipswich and was always looking forward to seeing them again.

At around the same time, Ann had an unusual dream in which Maria was buried under the floor of the family's barn, half a mile from their cottage home. It was known as the red barn due to its heavy red brick roof.

Ann's dream haunted her waking hours, and after she had the same dream a second night in a row, she spoke to Thomas about it, who replied that the only way to allay her dream was to go to the red barn and examine it.

On 19th April 1828, though Thomas was superstitious of Ann's dreams, he went to the red barn to check it. Upon noticing a dip in the exposed ground, he dug deeper with one of his mole catching tools and he hit something hard.

Body in a sack

Thomas didn't have to dig much deeper to find the horror that awaited him. Two feet down, he uncovered a sack with the decomposed skeletal remains of a female body. He saw her long hair and found a green handkerchief around her neck.

Praying to God it wasn't his daughter, he fled the barn and ran back to the cottage, where he asked

Ann if Maria had been wearing a handkerchief the day she left for Ipswich. Ann confirmed that Maria was wearing a green handkerchief that William had given her.

An inquest was held at a local inn, in Polstead, where Maria was identified by Ann. Though the body had decomposed, she was known to be missing a tooth, and her hair was recognisable, as were the clothing she had around her body.

The green handkerchief immediately implicated William in Maria's murder but he was nowhere to be seen. William had not returned to Polstead in many weeks and was found to have no connection to Ipswich. For a while, he had simply vanished into thin air.

William was born in 1803 and was two years younger than Maria when they met in 1826. He was the son of a local, wealthy farmer, and went by the nickname 'foxey' because of his cunning behaviour around other people, especially women.

He wanted to grow up and become a teacher but his father refused to financially support him in his dreams and as such, William became a petty criminal to get money, selling his father's pigs, forging cheques, and stealing pigs from other farms to sell on. He was known as a menace around the village.

Out of wedlock

William's father sent him to London in disgrace after selling his pigs and refused to have anything else to do with him. But in 1825, his father asked William to return home, because his brother, Thomas, had died, having drowned while walking across a frozen lake.

Over the next 18 months, William's other two brothers and his father all died from tuberculosis, and William was left alone with his mother to run the family farm. In 1826, when he was 22, he began a relationship with the then 24-year-old Maria, who had fallen for his charms and his wicked ways.

She wasn't unknown to him, as she had previously been in a relationship with his brother, Thomas. They had a child together, but the child had died in infancy at around the same time he had drowned in the lake.

Maria had one other child from another relationship with a man named Peter Matthews, who wasn't involved in the child's upbringing but would send money on a regular basis to help her care for the child, who she had named Thomas Henry.

Maria became pregnant by William in 1826, and gave birth to their child in 1827, when she was 25. William wanted commitment, he wanted to marry Maria, to legitimise their child and relationship, as having children out of wedlock in the 19th Century was still considered immoral and punishable by public whipping.

But two weeks later, tragedy struck, when the infant died in Maria's arms. William wrapped the body in a box and buried it in an unidentified location. William insisted that they marry, despite losing their child, and wanted it to happen sooner rather than later.

An evil squire

William went to the Marten cottage and suggested they meet at the red barn where they could hide out before eloping to Ipswich. He was able to convince Maria and her mother that the local constable might be investigating Maria's third child out of wedlock but Maria stayed inside the cottage.

On Friday 18th May 1827, William stormed into the Marten cottage and told Maria that they had to leave at once. He claimed he overheard that the local constable had obtained a warrant to prosecute Maria and that if found guilty, she would face a public lashing.

Maria agreed to elope to Ipswich with him, and later than night, ventured out to meet him at the red barn. William had already taken some of her belongings and clothing to the barn so she could get changed before eloping.

It was the last time Maria was seen alive. William claimed he had moved to Ipswich with her, and when he returned to the village to check in on his mother, he lied that Maria was doing well, but couldn't come home because of the constable's warrant.

11 months later, Ann's dreams led them to the discovery of Maria's body, realising she had only made it half a mile from their family home. It was discovered that William had not moved to Ipswich and had instead eloped to London.

A local constable and a London officer tracked William down and discovered he was running a girls boarding house in Brentford, West London. He had married his new wife, Mary Moore, who had answered his advertisement for love in The Times and Morning Herald newspapers. William was arrested while boiling eggs in the parlour.

Public trial

William denied ever knowing Maria or the Marten family but the officers were convinced of his guilt and charged him with the murder. The trial began back in Suffolk on 7th August 1828, at Shire Hall, where tickets to the court were put up for sale due to the large number of people who wanted to witness the trial.

It was written in newspapers of the day that the judges and court officials had to fight their way through the crowds just to get into the building. William pleaded not guilty to murder, despite the mounting evidence against him.

He had motive, evidence linking him to the scene, two pistols that were purchased the day of the murder, his false claim of not knowing Maria, witnesses who saw him leaving the village alone, and Maria's ten-year-old brother, George, who had seen him with a loaded pistol the night of the murder.

It was initially thought Maria had been stabbed through the eye due to abrasions on the skull. The decomposed wounds on her body suggested she had been shot but the coroner could not rule out death by strangulation due to the handkerchief around her neck. The cause of death was listed as inconclusive.

The motive, they claimed, was because William did not really want to marry Maria and was doing so because she allegedly had heat on him due to his previous criminal ventures. The prosecution stated that it was enough of a basis to convict him on.

William, however, told a different story. He agreed that he was waiting in the barn for Maria but that he had left after an argument. While he was walking away, he heard a gunshot, ran back to the barn and found her dead with one of his pistols beside her, claiming she had taken her own life.

A body through the ages

The jury didn't believe him but modern-day researchers suggest they may have been influenced by the public's belief he was the killer. William was convicted of Maria's murder and sentenced to death by hanging and then dissection.

While waiting for the gallows, William confessed to the death but claimed he had accidentally shot her in the eye as she was changing her clothes. Only five days after the trial began, on 11th August, William was led to the gallows in Bury St. Edmunds, and hung at noon in front of thousands of spectators. He confessed to the murder moments before he was executed.

The body was taken back to the courtroom and placed on a table where his stomach was cut open, exposing his innards. Newspaper reports of the time suggested 5,000 people queued up to see the body of William Corder.

His body was sent to Cambridge University where it was dissected in front of students and experimented on with batteries to prove contraction of muscle tissue. Several death masks were made, with one replica still on show at Moyse's Hall Museum in Bury St. Edmunds.

William's skin was tanned by a surgeon and subsequently used as a book binding for an account of the murder and trial. His skeleton was put back together and used as a teaching aid which was put on display at the Hunterian Museum in London, until 2004 when it was removed and cremated.

There is a theory that Ann Marten was having an affair with William and they planned to kill Maria so they could be with one another. Her 'dreams' were revenge for William getting married to another woman, so she had sought a way to punish him by exposing Maria's burial site. It has never been proven but has remained a discussion point ever since.

The murder of Maria Marten at the red barn has remained in the public domain ever since and has all the elements required of a murder in 19th Century England. Surviving items involved in the trial are on display at various museums or have been sold into private collections.

In the 200 years since the murder, the story of the red barn has been immortalised in plays, poems, ballads, films, books, songs, and editorial articles. It is as notorious today as it was almost 200 years ago.

The Burglars of Baker Street

A heist involving millionaire moles, underground tunnels, corrupt cops, MI5 censorship, a chicken takeaway, The Sweeney, and a conspiracy theory that reached all the way to the British royal family.

Without setting off a single alarm, a gang of robbers pulled off a notorious bank robbery in 1971, netting them nearly £3million, worth £40million today. The audacious plan involved them renting a leather goods shop two doors away from the Baker Street, London branch of Lloyds Bank.

They spent the weekends tunnelling under the neighbouring chicken takeaway and entered the bank through the floor of the vault. They made off with cash, jewels, and safety deposit boxes that may have included damning secrets involving the British royal family.

In 1970, career criminal Anthony Gavin came up with a plan to rob a bank. He had been inspired after reading the Arthur Conan Doyle story, 'The Red-Headed-League', a Sherlock Holmes tale involving a bank heist in which Holmes was waiting in the vault when burglars broke in.

Gavin was a 38-year-old photographer and former army PT instructor living in London at the time and began to put together his audacious plan. Having spent most of his life involved in petty crime, he already had acquaintances who would be interested in the plan.

Because he was so fanatical about The Red-Headed League, Gavin decided on the Baker Street branch of Lloyds, in a bizarre homage to the street where Sherlock Holmes had resided in the stories. But not only that, there were rumours on the streets the bank was a location that London's most powerful people would use.

Measuring the vault

Despite his connections to other criminals, Gavin first roped in his friend, car salesman Reg Tucker, who had no criminal history, but needed the money for his family. Together they set about planning the perfect bank robbery.

In December 1970, Tucker opened an account at the bank with a large deposit of £500, in order to stake it out. Two months later, he returned and rented a safety deposit box, as it was written in the bank's terms and conditions that customers should be left in private while visiting the vault.

Tucker visited the safety deposit box an additional 13 times in the months that followed but he wasn't there to check on any possessions, he was busy working. He measured the entire vault using the arms of his jacket and an umbrella he would take with him each time.

As the months rolled on, Tucker was able to measure and map the entire vault down to the closest inch, aided by square floor tiles that were uniformly the same size. He developed a perfect scaled drawing of the entire room with locations of the cabinets and boxes.

Gavin was said to be involved in a gang headed by Brian Reader, who later claimed he had nothing to do with the robbery, though evidence suggests otherwise. Reader convinced his friend, Bobby Mills, to be the lookout man in the weeks leading up to the robbery.

Reader and Gavin then employed another second-hand car salesman, Thomas Stephens, who also had no criminal record, to source the tools needed for the job, including a thermal lance, which is a tool used to burn through metal, and a 100-ton jack, used to lift heavy objects or keep them up.

Final piece of the plan

Then an opportunity opened that the gang couldn't turn down. They had been waiting for a nearby property to be put up for sale or let as they needed a location to start digging the tunnels. Only two doors along from the bank, a leather goods shop called Le Sac had suddenly gone out of business and closed its doors.

64-year-old antique and junk seller, Benjamin Wolfe, who knew some of the gang members, was convinced to join them in purchasing the lease for the shop. The owners of Le Sac sold Wolfe the lease for the entire property in May 1971 for £10,000, and the gang had the final piece of the puzzle.

The shop had a basement which they concluded was roughly the same depth as the vault. To maintain appearances, Gavin rented the shop legally from Wolfe and got to work.

At least five other people became involved in the plan, including a burglar-alarm expert named Mickey 'Skinny' Gervaise, and four unidentified members; an explosives expert, a security insider at the bank, a man nicknamed Little Legs, and another known as TH. Only Gavin, Tucker, Stephens, and Wolfe would go on to be convicted of the robbery.

Through their contact at the bank, they learned that a nearby construction project often caused false alarms, which meant the vault's vibration-based floor alarm would be turned off.

On August Bank Holiday weekend 1971, the team got to work digging through the basement wall, using the time the bank alarms were off. To avoid suspicion, they only worked weekends and ended up removing eight tons of dirt and waste which they dumped at the back of Le Sac.

Along the way, they bumped into a little problem – a chicken takeaway, that was between them and the bank. They hit the walls of the Chicken Inn, so had to dig deeper into the ground, using the wall as a guide. Then they dug under the takeaway, using its basement floor as the ceiling of the tunnel.

By the time they hit the floor of the vault, the tunnel was 12 metres (40ft) long, and led to a two-metre squared cavity underneath it. Because they used existing structures as the walls and ceiling of the tunnel, it had proved to be safe and secure.

The walkie-talkie job

On Friday 10th September 1971, the lookout man went to the top of a building opposite the bank and had his walkie-talkie ready, allowing him to keep in contact with the gang. The robbery got underway but it went wrong immediately.

The idea behind the 100-ton jack was to force a hole into the three-foot thick concrete of the vault floor. They placed the jack on railway sleepers and turned it on but instead of pushing through the concrete above, it sank into a hidden well beneath them.

After the thermal lance failed to made a dent in the concrete, they decided to use explosives. A day later on the Saturday, they set off explosives under the vault floor, that were co-ordinated with the movement of traffic above. They managed to then chisel out a small hole into the vault itself.

At 11pm on that Saturday night, amateur radio enthusiast Robert Rowlands was scanning the airwaves from his flat in Wimpole Street, 400 metres away, when he picked up an unusual local broadcast. It was two men with cockney accents talking over the citizen band wavelength, which was illegal to use at the time in the UK.

He realised he was listening to the escapades of two criminals, who were discussing whether they should continue for the night or return in the early hours. Their mention of security, criminal lingo, and the plan led Rowlands to phone the police.

As it was late on a Saturday night when most bars were turfing people out on the street, the police commonly received calls from drunken people playing pranks or messing around. They told Rowlands that if it was serious that he should record the conversation – which he did.

He managed to record over an hour's worth of audio, mostly of an argument between those in the tunnel and the lookout, who was moaning how tired he was. At 2am, Rowlands phoned Scotland Yard directly, instead of the local police, and they sent members of the Flying Squad (also known as The Sweeney) to his house.

They confirmed a robbery was taking place or had taken place. At 8.30am, the conversation between the lookout and robbers inside the vault restarted, and a few minutes later, the gang confirmed on radio that the robbery had been completed but they would be sorting through the deposit boxes before leaving.

Surveillance

The Sweeney lambasted the police but ordered them to contact local bank staff and security firms to open up their branches early to look for signs of a break-in. Police visited the Baker Street branch of Lloyds at 3.30pm on the Sunday but couldn't access the vault as it was time-locked. It was discovered later that the gang were inside the vault at the time, sifting through their loot.

Bank staff discovered they had been robbed on the Monday morning. Police swarmed the area, discovered the tunnel led to the leather shop, and ultimately collected 800 pieces of evidence. 268 safety deposit boxes had been opened including one owned by the Lord Chancellor.

Police decided to release the audio recordings to the press on the Monday afternoon, which led to the incident being referred to as the walkie-talkie job. They held a press-conference saying they were looking for four men and a woman, who was supposedly being used by a higher power to control the gang, though it was never proven.

Eight owners of safety deposit boxes refused to allow their names being handed over to police, which would later lead to multiple conspiracy theories. Within three days, police latched onto Wolfe, as he was the new owner of the Le Sac shop, along with Gavin who had rented it.

The police then surveilled the gang for four weeks, hoping to identify all the members before arresting them. In October 1971, surveillance teams watched Tucker hand over a bag full of cash to Abdullah Hashan Gangji and his nephew Ackbar Mohammad Ali Gangji.

Realising the time had come to arrest them, police swooped in, picked up Tucker and the two Gangji's, and arrested Gavin, Wolfe, and Stephens at the same time in separate raids. The bank offered a £30,000 reward for information leading to further arrests of individuals involved.

D-Notice

The two Gangji's were charged with handling stolen goods but claimed they working for a Swiss-based financial institution who purchased British notes in cash. They were found not guilty at their trial and released with no further charges.

Gavin, Tucker, and Stephens pleaded guilty and were sentenced to 12 years a piece. Wolfe pleaded not guilty on the basis that he had signed the lease for Le Sac to Gavin and had only returned once to pick up the post, claiming he was shocked to have heard the news of the robbery.

A jury found him guilty of colluding to rob the bank and was sentenced to eight years in prison. In 1977, 138 security box owners affected by the robbery sued Lloyds for a combined total of close to £1million. The case went to the High Court, but for an undisclosed reason, the judge adjourned the case and it never reopened.

Because of the pausing of the case, rumours began to do the rounds. The first was that, in an unusual intervention at the time of the robbery, the British Government and the MI5 issued a D-Notice in relation to the case.

Also known as a DSMA-Notice (Defence and Security Media Advisory Notice), it is an official request to news editors not to release information on a subject for reasons of national security. However, with news outlets running stories of the walkie-talkie job, it seemed unlikely, unless the request was for one specific element – a member of the British royal family.

Conspiracies

This led to another rumour that one of the safety deposit boxes contained photographs of Princess

Margaret and the gangland criminal John Bindon. According to an unknown source, the pair were photographed cavorting with each other but it has never been proven.

Another claimed there were photographs in one of the boxes of a Tory MP abusing children. Those who believe the theory claim the D-Notice was issued to protect the Government, and that the MI5 orchestrated the robbery to retrieve the photos.

A few years later, a strip-club owner, James Humphreys, suggested that corrupt police officers had stolen at least £1million worth of loot as their share of the burglary. One of the unidentified members of the gang, known as TH, was suggested to be a contact of Alec Eist, a known corrupt Detective Inspector in Scotland Yard for over 20 years.

The so-called leader of the gang from afar, Brian Header, was involved in the now infamous 2015 Hatton Garden safe deposit theft which carried a close resemblance to the Baker Street burglary.

The four men convicted of the robbery were all released within ten years. Not much is known about what happened to them after that, with suggestions that Gavin went on to have a successful career in software development. To fuel the conspiracy theories, 800 pages of information relating to the case became classified and locked for 100 years until 2071.

Despite the theories, release of the people involved, and a film called The Bank Job, starring Jason Statham, only 10% of the loot was ever recovered, meaning someone, somewhere, became very rich off the back of it.

The Keyworth Murder

A confident killer murdered a 16-year-old girl and escaped justice for 25 years until advancements in DNA technology captured him, in the first case to be profiled on Crimewatch.

On the last afternoon of her young life, 16-year-old trainee hairdresser Colette Aram spent the time preparing and baking cakes at her family home in Keyworth, Nottinghamshire, a large village six miles from the centre of Nottingham.

At 8pm on 30th October 1983, Colette left home to visit her boyfriend's house. He normally picked her up from her house but his car had been taken off the road as it required work. The 1.5mile walk normally took about 25 minutes, but by 10pm, when Colette hadn't arrived, the alarm was raised.

Phone calls were made between her boyfriend and family before they realised something bad must have happened. Fearing Colette had become involved in an accident, her family and friends began searching for her along the route but the cold bite of the October night proved a hindrance.

Police put out a missing person's report and suspected she may have visited a friend's house but all her friend's told them they had not seen her. Though her family thought an accident may have happened, they were not prepared for the truth.

At 9am on Halloween morning, Colette's naked body was found in a field a mile away from where she had been abducted. She had been raped and strangled to death, with her body posed in a sexually provocative manner.

Crimewatch

When the missing persons case turned into a murder investigation, police increased their manpower and began seeking information from locals. Colette had last been seen ten minutes after leaving her home when she stopped and talked to a group of friends.

Ten minutes after, a resident in a nearby house remembered hearing a woman scream but was unsure if it was kids messing around or a genuine cry for help. The resident remembered hearing a car drive off immediately after.

Crime scene investigators collected as much evidence from the scene of the crime as they could, which would help them in the future when DNA technology had advanced. At the time, police had little to go on, with only minimal forensic evidence, no direct eye-witnesses to the abduction, or a suspect.

The case went cold quickly much to the public's anger and put Keyworth on the map for all the wrong reasons. Nine months later, in June 1984, the BBC released the first episode of a crime reconstruction and appeal programme called Crimewatch.

Colette's murder was notable for being the very first case to be featured on the show. The format of Crimewatch was to reconstruct as much information of a crime as possible, in the way that was agreed upon by police.

As a result of the programme, Nottinghamshire Police received 400 calls, some of which claimed to have seen a car leaving the village at high speed. The programme allowed police to eliminate over 1,500 suspects.

But aside from wiping the suspect list, and various other tips, most of the calls led nowhere and the killer had seemingly got away with it. The case was run a second time on Crimewatch's 20th Anniversary show in 2004, but again, the case was already as cold as ice.

Never say never

The killer was 25-year-old Paul Stewart Hutchinson, a youth worker who had a liking for young girls. On the day of the murder, he had spent hours in a shed near a riding school close to the village, waiting for girls to start walking home alone.

His heinous plan was to lure one of them into the shed and rape them. He had already approached two girls that morning who told their families a man had acted strangely around them. It was reported to police only after the murder became public knowledge, but by that point, Hutchinson was long gone.

When he failed to select a victim, he stole a Ford Fiesta and drove around the country lanes, hoping to find a girl walking out in the darkness alone. At around 8.20pm, he pulled up next to Colette and proceeded to speak to her before jumping out of the car and abducting her at knifepoint.

He bundled her into the back seat of the car and smashed a bottle over her head before driving to a secluded location and raping her. He then hit her with the bottle multiple times before strangling her to death.

After killing her, he moved the body to the middle of a nearby field and posed her body, for reasons that never became known. Many suspect he was attempting to trick police into thinking he was a serial killer and that if he posed the body a certain way, the police would be looking for someone else.

Hutchinson didn't stop there, and out of a morbid curiosity, had returned to the village to watch the police investigation amidst the supposed anonymity of the crowds on 31st October, while wearing a Halloween mask.

A few days later, he sent a letter to police that read; *'No one knows what I look like. That is why you have not got me. You will never get me.'* For many years, the letter proved to be true but under the old adage of 'never say never', justice would finally catch up with him, 25 years later.

Unusual hit on the DNA database

To cover his tracks, Hutchinson told his family he had cancer, and shaved his head, blaming it on chemotherapy, which was a lie. In the years that followed, Hutchinson believed he had escaped justice, and was able to work with children with learning disabilities.

In 2008, and because of advances in DNA technology, police were able to use the carefully protected forensic evidence from the crime scene and put together a DNA profile of the killer. At the same time they appealed for members of the public to report anyone they thought might have been involved in the murder.

The appeal didn't work but in June 2008 the DNA database returned a hit – which immediately didn't make sense. A man called Jean-Paul was arrested on a traffic offense and a DNA swab was taken at the police station.

His DNA was a near-identical match to the murder suspect profile drawn up by forensics. The police had their man, after 25 years, they could finally seek justice for Colette's murder, except, Jean-Paul had been born five years after the murder took place which instantly ruled him out.

The DNA match provided police with the clues they needed to solve the case and learned that Jean-Paul was the son of Paul Stewart Hutchinson, which is why the DNA profiles were so similar. Police arrested the then 50-year-old Hutchinson at his home the same day.

But Hutchinson, ever the confident murderer, had already developed a story to get the police off his scent. He claimed that the true suspect was his own brother who had passed away six months earlier and had been cremated.

Fortunately, for police, the hospital where his brother was staying before his death had taken blood samples, which didn't match the DNA profile of the killer. Hutchinson still pleaded not guilty but changed his plea to guilty on the advice of his lawyer.

The passage of time

In January 2010, 26 years after Colette's murder, Hutchinson was convicted and sentenced to a minimum of 25 years, one for each of the years he believed he had gotten away with murder. A week after his murder, Crimewatch returned to the case.

With the new evidence and killer behind bars, Crimewatch put out a new show featuring the case. In it, they were able to retrospectively look at the inconsistencies with their original programming and point out errors that had been made.

They also discovered errors in the media's reporting of the murder, including that Hutchinson was a psychology graduate, which he wasn't. Some of the inconsistencies in their programme may have resulted in Hutchinson getting away with the murder at the time.

Crimewatch was a vital investigatory and appeal component of major crimes in the UK, but due to declining viewership, the BBC cancelled the programme in 2017. Various spin-offs continue to run on broadcast television.

Ten months after his conviction, and suffering from depression, Hutchinson took an overdose of prescription medication and was found dead in his cell on 10th October 2010.

For Colette's family it was a heavy blow as it appeared Hutchinson had chosen not to live out his punishment. They were also hoping he would one day confess to the murder and explain why he had taken away their loved one, as he had never given a reason.

Colette's case shows that despite the passage of time, justice will inevitably find a way, and those who have committed historical crimes will forever be looking over their shoulders.

The Cage Beneath Monster Mansion

Known as the real Hannibal the Cannibal, Britain's most dangerous prisoner was confined to a specially built glass isolation cage in the basement of one of the country's most notorious prisons.

Considered one of Britain's most dangerous prisoners, Robert John Maudsley killed four people, three of them while in maximum security facilities. To protect other inmates, a special glass cell was constructed in the basement of HMP Wakefield which became known as The Cage.

Born in 1953, Maudsley had 11 siblings growing up and spent most of his time in an orphanage due to the broken relationship with his parents. When he was eight, Maudsley was physically and sexually abused by his parents.

He had been raped as a child and didn't escape the rotating door of abuse until social services stepped in and removed him from his parents' care when he was 10. His broken childhood led him to a deep drug addiction in his teenage years, which inevitably sent him down a spiral of self-abuse.

To subsidise his addiction, he turned to prostitution, and moved to London when he was 16. He attempted suicide on many occasions, which led to him receiving temporary psychiatric care, where he was diagnosed with a deep-rooted depression.

He told doctors he was hearing voices telling him to go back and kill his parents, which he later claimed would have been the right thing to do. '*If I had killed my parents in 1970, none of these people need have died.*' – Maudsley

In 1974, a punter named John Farrell picked Maudsley up for sex but he had darker fantasies he wanted to share with the then 19-year-old. Farrell showed Maudsley photographs of the children he had sexually abused.

Enraged by images of child abuse which had brought back memories of his own upbringing, Maudsley killed Farrell by strangling him with a garotte, stabbing him multiple times, and hitting him over the head with a hammer.

The brain eater

Not long after, Maudsley surrendered to police and asked for psychiatric help. It became clear to the authorities that Maudsley was not only a danger to others but to himself, having attempted suicide multiple times before Farrell's murder.

Because of his personal history, psychiatric issues, and extenuating circumstances, in 1977 he was found unfit to stand trial and sent to Broadmoor Hospital, a high-security psychiatric facility, which has been home to some of the country's most notorious criminals, including The Yorkshire Ripper, Charles Bronson, Ronnie Kray, and the Freddy Krueger Killer.

While there, he and another patient, John Cheeseman, locked themselves in a prison office with a known convicted paedophile, David Francis. They tied him up with electrical cord and tortured him over a period of almost ten hours, before Maudsley strangled him to death.

When they surrendered, one of the guards who was first into the room claimed that Francis's head had been cracked open and a spoon was sticking out of his skull. It was widely reported that a piece of his brain was missing, and that Maudsley had cannibalised it.

Though it remains a point of contention, it has never been conclusively proven either way whether Maudsley had eaten part of the brain. As the story began to do the rounds, Maudsley earned the unfortunate nickname of Hannibal the Cannibal, despite reports to the contrary that the cannibal aspect of the killing was false.

Monster Mansion

Maudsley was convicted of manslaughter and not murder due to diminished responsibility but was deemed to be of relatively sane mind. As such, he was sent to Wakefield Prison, commonly known as Monster Mansion due to it's unfortunate roster of dangerous criminals.

Inmates known to have been resident at Monster Mansion include Harold Shipman (Doctor Death), Ian Huntley, Colin Ireland, Robert Black, Ian Watkins (former frontman of Lost Prophets), and USSR spy Klaus Fuchs, among countless others.

Other prisoners in Wakefield were already aware of Maudsley's reputation and he was given the nickname 'Spoons' due to the story of the spoon sticking out of Francis's skull.

On July 28th 1978, Robert Maudsley told other inmates that he was going to kill two people that day. His case is a unique one in that he would kill more people in prison than he did on the outside.

On that fateful day, Maudsley lured wife-killer Salney Darwood, into his cell. He tied a garotte around his neck and smashed Darwood's head repeatedly into the wall. He hid the body under his bed and tried to lure other prisoners into his cell.

When no one came in, he prowled the prison and walked into the cell of Bill Roberts before stabbing him to death with a shiv, a homemade blade. After having killed the two men, he calmly walked into a prison guard's office and placed the bloody handmade weapon on the table.

He looked up at the guard and said; *'there'll be two short when it comes to the next roll call.'* Maudsley surrendered to the guards and was transferred to solitary confinement to await trial, where he was convicted of both murders and sentenced to life at Wakefield Prison.

The cannibal and the cage

Maudsley had killed three people while inside a high security psychiatric facility and a maximum security prison. He was considered such a dangerous criminal that the prison service decided to build a unique isolation cage to house him.

In 1983, a specially-constructed cell was built in the basement of Wakefield Prison, where Maudsley has resided ever since. The glass cage, 5.5metres by 4.5metres, has bulletproof windows and an entire team of prison officers assigned to watch him.

In order to access The Cage you would have to go through an astonishing 17 locked steel doors. The only furniture is a cardboard table and chair, a bed made up of a thin mattress on a concrete slab, and a toilet and sink bolted to the floor.

The Cage, though rarely seen, has been likened to the Hannibal Lecter cell in The Silence of the

Lambs movie. Thomas Harris, the author of the Hannibal Lecter series, wrote The Silence of the Lambs in 1988, five years after Maudsley's cage had been built.

He wrote the first Hannibal Lecter book, Red Dragon, in 1981, four years after the story of Maudsley eating part of a brain. Harris based some elements of the character of Hannibal Lecter on Maudsley's case, specifically the cannibal part of the story and the glass isolation cell.

Unsurprisingly, this led to Maudsley gaining the moniker of Hannibal the Cannibal in the British press, something which has never gone away. Maudsley is also known to have high intelligence and a passion for high art and classical music. Those who are allowed to be in close contact with him, have long claimed that he is a gentleman to be around, much like Hannibal Lecter.

An isolated life

Maudsley remains in The Cage for 23 hours a day and is fed through a glass drawer on the front. When he is allowed his one hour a day for exercise, he is escorted to the yard by no less than six prison officers and is banned from interacting with any other inmate.

Unsurprisingly, there are some people who see Maudsley as a hero vigilante, who killed paedophiles and wife beaters. There is still an active campaign to move him out of The Cage where he has resided for most of his life.

His family have long claimed that his isolation is detrimental to any rehabilitation and that he lives in a cloud of depression. In 2000, his defence team appealed to relax his solitary confinement measures or that he be allowed to end his own life with a cyanide capsule. Both were denied.

In the 1990s, notorious inmate Charles Bronson, who had also come from Broadmoor, decided to try and befriend Maudsley by sending him a watch via a prison guard. Maudsley told the guard to throw it out with the rubbish, leading to Bronson calling Maudsley an *'ungrateful bastard.'*

He went on to say that he hoped to one day bump into Maudsley and that he wouldn't need a blade to overpower him. He ended his tirade with, *'nobody rips my heart out or eats my brain, especially a nutcase like Bob Maudsley.'*

In 2010, Maudsley petitioned officials to let him play board games with guards to pass the time. His request was denied because of the murders committed behind bars, and the suspicion that Maudsley was still violent.

Their beliefs were backed up in March 2022, when the then 68-year-old Maudsley claimed in a letter to his nephew that he would kill again the moment he was released, and that he was content to remain in solitary confinement for the rest of his life.

Britain's most dangerous prisoner

There are some mixed beliefs as to whether Maudsley should be labelled as a serial killer, but by any classification, Maudsley *is* a serial killer. Whether he is a vigilante or not depends on how much one believes Maudsley had killed because his victims were child abusers or wife beaters, something which he hated.

Though some journalists and researchers write about the tragedy of Maudsley and how he was driven to kill out of revenge for the 'true' bad people in the world, it remains a fact that he has killed four men, three behind bars.

His childhood was tragic, forged in the darkness of abuse, lack of foundation, and hate over love. In his adult life, Maudsley chose to kill four others, whether out of revenge, hate, or circumstance.

Either way, he was deemed to be Britain's most dangerous prisoner and remains in the basement of Monster Mansion, feared by guards and other inmates. His case has shone a light on long term prisoners who wish to end their own life and if the law might be changed to allow it but there has been no progress since 2000.

No photo of Maudsley exists past 1983 and no images of The Cage have ever been released to the public. No one really knows if there truly was a spoon sticking out the skull of one of his victims but the legend perpetuates to this day.

If the prison service have deemed Maudsley dangerous enough to remain isolated in The Cage, and that Maudsley himself claims he will kill again if ever released, then maybe Maudsley is where he needs to be.

The Black Panther Serial Killer

With over 400 thefts, 19 post office robberies, four murders, and countless assaults to his name, the Black Panther was Britain's most prolific criminal, known for the disturbing death of a kidnapped girl.

By the 1970s, post office robberies in Britain were on the increase, as criminals turned their attention away from banks to focus on mostly rural locations with minimal to zero security. Post office's general level of security was simply a sales counter between the customer and staff.

Donald Nielson was one of the more known post office robbers who hit dozens of establishments from 1971 to 1974. His case stands out above many others, as he murdered four people, including a young girl he kidnapped for ransom.

Nielson was born Donald Nappey in Bradford in August 1936 and quickly turned to crime. In

1947, when he was 10, Nielson's mother died of cancer and he was left alone with a father who didn't want him. At the same time, he was being bullied in school over his surname, which he hated.

He entered the criminal lifestyle a year later, aged 11, when he broke into a shop to rob the cash register, but was caught red-handed by police, who let him off with a caution due to his age, unaware of what the future was to hold.

When he was 17, he was conscripted into the army as part of the British National Service law that required healthy males to serve in the armed forces for 18 months and remain on the reserve list for four years. A year later in 1955, he married the love of his life, Irene Tate, a woman two years older than he was. She convinced him to leave the army as soon as his 18-month service had come to an end. But Nielson relished the army lifestyle which had encouraged his love of guns and other weapons.

He left the army for his wife and set up a business making sheds at their home in Bradford. In 1960, they give birth to a daughter named Kathryn, and Nielson changed his surname to rid himself of his embarrassing family name and prevent similar bullying to his daughter.

Prolific burglar

The new surname was chosen because he had recently purchased a taxi business from a man named Nielson and liked the sound of it. It was a coincidence that he would be later confused with Dennis Nielsen, another serial killer who was active from 1978.

When Nielson was 29, in 1965, he was drawn back to his life of crime and became addicted to carrying out burglaries. It was estimated he had committed over 400 burglaries from 1965 to when he was finally caught in 1975.

He was aggrieved each time, as the proceeds from the crimes were small but knew that if he escalated too quickly that the police would be on to him. In the early days, he adapted his method of burglary to what the news was saying about him.

When he worked out that police had established a pattern of behaviour, he would change it up. On many occasions, he stole a radio and left it on the pavement near the property. When he read about the radio connection in the newspapers, he included a different calling card, such as leaving a tap on, or moving items in the house around.

In November 1970, realising the minimal returns were getting him nowhere, he broke into a large family home in Dewsbury, West Yorkshire, and stole two shotguns from the well-off family, including a large amount of ammunition.

During the year that followed, his burglaries became more violent as he fought homeowners and restrained others so he could get what he wanted. On every occasion, he wore a black mask and black clothing, and sometimes put on an accent in an attempt to outwit police. Before he was known as The Black Panther, the press referred to him as The Phantom, or Handy Andy.

Post office loot

In early 1971, he used one of the shotguns to rob a sub-post office in Barnsley and escaped with a little over £3,000, worth £50,000 today. Seeing the success of the raid, he robbed another post office in Rotherham where he made off with almost £4,000.

A few months later, he burgled a house in Cheshire and stole two automatic pistols, three rifles, and bags full of ammunition. He chose certain houses as he discovered they were either farmers or hunters, and as such were likely to have firearms on the premises.

Shortly after raiding the house, he held up a sub-post office in Mansfield, and made off with nearly £3,000. Nielson was beginning to amass a large amount of cash but couldn't escape the thrill of the crime.

In February 1972, he broke into a small post office in Heywood, Lancashire, which was attached to a small family home. The house and post office owner, Leslie Richardson, awoke in the middle of the night to find Nielson standing beside his bed with a shotgun.

Richardson, who had also served in the army, leapt out of bed to fight with the intruder. Nielson fought back and broke bones in Richardson's feet by stamping on them, before shooting him in the leg and eloping empty-handed. Richardson and his wife survived the attack.

Escalation to murder

From 1971 to 1974, he held up 19 post offices at gunpoint, and made off with thousands of pounds each time. By this point, the press had begun referring to him as The Black Panther, because a witness remarked on his speed, which was as fast as a panther, and the fact he was wearing all black clothing and a black mask.

The first murder to be linked to Nielson happened in February 1974, when he robbed a sub-post office in Harrogate. Owner Donald Skepper confronted Nielson, who lifted his shotgun and blasted him in the chest, killing him instantly.

Seven weeks later, he raided a post office in Baxenden, Lancashire and shot dead postmaster Derek Astin. Two months after Astin's death, and with the police hot on his trail, Nielson continued to carry out robberies and burglaries across Yorkshire, resulting in another murder.

In November 1974, Nielson robbed a post office in Langley, West Midlands, that belonged to Sidney Grayland and his wife Margaret, who lived on the premises. When Sidney attempted to fight Nielson off, he was shot dead. Nielson then beat Margaret with the butt of the shotgun to within an inch of her life. Fortunately, she survived the attack but was left with life-changing injuries.

Not content with having robbed tens of thousands of pounds and killing three people, Nielson came up with a plan that would go on to shock, not just Yorkshire, but the whole of the country.

The Whittle kidnapping

A few years earlier, Nielson had read a news story about a 17-year-old girl named Lesley Whittle, who had been left £82,000 by her father, George, in his will to avoid estate taxes, worth £1.3million today. George had been a coach business owner and had amassed a large fortune off the back of it.

On 14th January 1975, after having planned it for many years, Nielson broke into Whittle's large home in Shropshire by cutting a telephone line connected to the house, which he suspected was a burglar alarm, then crept into the property through the garage

Though he had originally intended to kidnap Lesley's mother, Dorothy, as she too had been left a fortune, he instead decided to kidnap Lesley when he came across her room first. He gagged her as Dorothy was asleep in the next room, having taken sleeping pills the evening before.

Nielson kidnapped Lesley, who was the same age as his daughter, and tied her up on the back seat of car, before holding her captive, hoping to pick up a hefty ransom. He had left a ransom note on Lesley's bed demanded £50,000 for her return with detailed instructions of where to leave the cash and not to involve the police, thinking it would have been easy for the Whittle family to follow.

He drove Lesley to Bathpool Park in Kidsgrove, Staffordshire, 45 miles away. He led her to a deep drainage shaft connected to a nearby reservoir, before climbing down with her to a small platform, 16 metres below the surface.

He put a hood over her head, stripped her naked and secured her to the platform with wire around her neck. He provided her with a small mattress and sleeping bag and left her in the freezing darkness before going home to his wife and daughter.

Botched ransom drop

Dorothy found the ransom note the next morning and phoned her step-son and Lesley's brother, Ronald Whittle. When he didn't pick up, she jumped in her car and sped over to the home that he shared with his wife, Gaynor, before bringing them back to the Whittle house.

Despite the ransom note stating not to contact the police, Ronald made the decision to call them.

The note stated that one of the Whittle family members was to wait for a phone call at a public telephone box beside a shopping centre in Kidderminster that evening.

The police and press became involved in a big way and were ultimately responsible for a serious of errors that messed up the ransom delivery. Some journalists realised the local police were involved in something big, uncovered the story and released it to news channels the same evening.

As midnight came, and Nielson hadn't called the phone box, both the police and press feared the worst. Then at 1am on January 16th, Nielson phoned and played a tape message with Lesley's voice, claiming she was okay but stated that a Whittle family member should go to a second phone box where there were instructions hidden behind it.

24 hours later, in the early hours of the 17th, Ronald Whittle drove to the second phone box with £50,000 in a suitcase but got lost and went 1.5 miles off course due to police not giving him the correct directions.

Half hour later, he reached the destination and found the note that instructed him to walk to the next lane in Bathpool Park, flash the car lights, then look out for torch light at the end of the lane.

He followed the instructions, but there was no sign of Nielson, even after Ronald exited the vehicle and shouted. Nielson had been spooked by a routine patrol car that had passed near the lane just minutes before Ronald arrived.

The blame was placed squarely on the police for not changing the route of the car, as the officer driving had no idea about the drop. Police searched the park the next day but didn't find any evidence, missing the drain shaft where Lesley was being kept. As a result of the mess up, they ordered a media blackout.

Horrific death

The same night of the failed ransom drop, a security guard called Gerald Smith had been shot six times in the back and was recovering in hospital. A car was located near the scene that had a tape recorder with Lesley's voice on it, and other evidence linking to Nielson but West Midlands police didn't find out until one week later.

As the hunt for the kidnapper went into a second week, forensic experts confirmed that the evidence found in the car, and the bullets that were pulled out of Gerald, matched those used in The Black Panther robberies and murders.

On 6th March, a school headmaster informed police that a pupil had handed him a note that mentioned dropping a suitcase into a hole, along with a flashlight wedged into the grill of a drainage shaft. Police then descended on Bathpool Park, a location they had already searched.

When gas experts confirmed the shafts were safe to open, police entered them. 14 metres down in the third shaft, they found a tape recorder on a flat surface which suggested Nielson had used the shaft to hide Lesley.

On the third landing, 16 metres down, they found the mattress and sleeping bag, but below the landing, Lesley's nude and decomposing body was hanging from the steel wire by her neck, with her toes only six inches from the bottom of the shaft. When the body was found, the lead investigator, Chief Superintendent Bob Booth, was demoted to a street officer for the succession of failures.

There were two theories relating to Lesley's death, one that Nielson had re-entered the shaft to push her to her death, and another that he never returned and she either took her own life or died in an accident when she fell.

An autopsy suggested she had died from vagal inhibition, which occurs when pressure is placed on the vagus nerve in the neck, causing the brain to slow down the heart. In Lesley's case, her heart stopped altogether, leading to her death.

They also discovered she had not consumed any food or water for three days prior to her death, due to her stomach and intestines being empty, and may have been alive for up to seven days before she died.

A class apart

In December 1975, 11 months after Lesley's death which had shocked the nation, two officers on road duty were sitting in their car in Mansfield, when they spotted a suspicious looking man carrying a holdall. They approached him to search the bag but he pulled out a shotgun and ordered them back into the car.

They had unknowingly been accosted by Nielson, who ordered them to drive to another town six miles away. When they approached a junction beside a fish and chip takeaway, the officer behind the wheel slammed on the brakes but the gun went off, hitting him in the hand.

The car came to a screeching halt and the other officer called for help. Two men who were queuing at the takeaway ran to the police car to assist and eventually they all overpowered Nielson. They dragged him to iron railings on the side of the road and handcuffed him as back-up arrived.

After all the evidence had emerged, Nielson was charged with four murders, multiple robberies, theft of weapons, kidnapping, and assault. In Lesley's case, Nielson pleaded not guilty to murder, but instead pleaded guilty to manslaughter.

At his trial in July 1976, Nielson was found guilty of Lesley's murder and told by the judge that the *'enormity of his crimes put him in a class apart from almost all other convicted murderers in recent years.'*

He was sentenced to life for the murder of Lesley, and another four life sentences for the three other murders and attack on Margaret Grayland. He received an additional 21 years for the kidnapping, 10 years for blackmail, and another 30 years for theft and weapons offences.

It was clear that Nielson would never leave prison alive and would meet the end of his days inside. Gerald the security guard died of his wounds one year later but a conviction was not pursued as it wouldn't have changed the ultimate outcome of a whole life tariff.

In 2008, aged 72, Nielson appealed to lower his sentence but it was refused by the Home Secretary, and the whole life tariff was upheld. In 2011, Nielson died in hospital of natural causes, and for the hundreds of families affected by his crimes, they were finally able to breathe a sigh of relief.

The Jolly Farmer Explosion

A giant explosion levelled a quaint English pub and left one person dead, but as the rubble was cleared, a survivor was found, and a realisation the explosion was no accident.

Blacknest in Hampshire, England, is such a small village that before you know you're in it, you're already on the road out. But Blacknest, which is in the civil parish of Binsted, harbours a mystery that has never been solved.

On 5th December 1989, the village was preparing for Christmas, decorations were hanging in the resident's windows, Santa was preparing for his visit, and the local pub was about to become ground zero for an almighty explosion.

The Jolly Farmer was a local and typically English pub that hosted many of the residents of Blacknest, and those travelling in from the wider community. Its quaint location, surrounded by fields and lush countryside, was one of its big selling points.

By 2am, the pub had closed, the customers and staff had gone home for the night, and only the bar manager Richard Dean, and the second chef Clifford Howes, remained, finishing the clean-up for the night.

Half hour later, a giant explosion destroyed the pub, killing Clifford, and leaving Richard fighting for his life. The explosion was no accident.

Sword in the stone

The blast was so large it was heard across Hampshire and reached houses many miles away. Emergency services were called to the scene and discovered the Jolly Farmer had been completely destroyed, with smoke billowing from the mound of rubble.

The pub was only identifiable by its metal sign and a chimney that remained standing. Debris from the explosion was found over 100 metres away. As the morning light broke through the canopy, beer barrels and Christmas decorations were found in the fields surrounding it.

The emergency services first assumed that no-one had been inside due to the lateness of the hour, however, as they began searching, they found an arm sticking out of the rubble, pointing towards the dawn sky.

Miraculously, Richard had survived, and the rescuer who found him said his arm sticking through the rubble was like the sword in the stone from the Arthurian legend. But when they got him out, he was not in a good way. His clothes had melted to his skin by the heat of the explosion and a quarter of his body had been burned.

Clifford, who lodged at the pub, did not survive. He had been asleep in the middle section of the building when the explosion happened. As the entire pub fell on top of him, he crashed down into the cellar, crushed by beams and mortar. Unable to escape, he was burned alive in the fire.

His body wasn't found until the early afternoon of the 5th, when rescuers finally cleared a path to the cellar. They were only pushed to keep digging when the landlord, Arthur Thompkins, and his wife, told them that Clifford lodged there. If they hadn't continued, Clifford may never have been found.

After the rubble was searched, local detectives and police investigated the ruins of the pub. After smelling gasoline all over the place, and finding the remains of a homemade wick, investigators realised the Jolly Farmer had been destroyed on purpose, and the site became a crime scene.

No accident

The investigation concluded that someone had deliberately targeted the Jolly Farmer. Just before

2am on that fateful morning, someone had taken the effort to professionally cut the phone lines connected to the pub, though to this day, the reasons behind it remain unclear, and an unnecessary added step.

A large amount of petrol had been poured through the wooden cellar doors at the side of the pub. The cellar floor would have been an inch deep in petrol to have caused an explosion of that scale. In the cellar, like all pubs, the beer kegs, the gas lines, and the supplies were stacked up, ready for the Christmas period.

The wick that was discovered in the rubble was deemed not to be the cause of the explosion, as it had burned out. The person or persons who poured the petrol in the cellar would have tried to use the wick to light it. Ultimately, the explosion was caused by an electric dehumidifier.

When it sensed vapour in the air of the cellar, it automatically kicked into life. The spark ignited the vapour, which spread to the petrol, and caused an instant explosion large enough to be heard miles away.

If Clifford and Richard had smelled the gasoline or realised the phone lines had been cut then they may have exited the pub before the explosion. As it was, one life was ended, and the other changed forever.

Almost immediately, the police struggled with the ensuing investigation. They had theories, ranging from an upset customer targeting the pub, to a deliberate act by gangs. But there was nothing to go on, no forensics, no real evidence, and no motive.

The other Jolly Farmer's

The Jolly Farmer's staff and landlord had no enemies and no reason for someone to attack them, beyond the realms of usual drunkenness. The person who had attacked the pub had a clear plan in place, and a drunken patron was ruled out straight away.

It was a quiet little pub in the middle of nowhere, building up to primetime custom over the Christmas period. The landlord, Arthur, reasoned that it may have been mistaken identity, as there were 21 pubs in England with the same name, and seven in the county of Hampshire alone.

Investigators spoke to the landlords of the other Jolly Farmer's and found no reason why they would have been targeted themselves. The whole investigation was ended on the conclusion that it was unsolvable, despite it becoming a murder enquiry.

One witness claimed to have spotted a car speeding away from the explosion but the car was never identified. It remains plausible that a vehicle would have been needed to carry the amount of petrol used in the attack. Why Clifford or Richard didn't approach the car, if it was involved, remains another mystery, unless the car was simply passing at the time of the explosion.

If the dehumidifier hadn't sparked into life, then it's possible the explosion may not have occurred. The wick was set alight by the arsonist, and they may have been driving away expecting it to just catch fire. But the wick burned out, and instead of a fire, they got an explosion.

Discomforting twist of fate

In 2003, the case was reviewed using new DNA technology but no new leads came to light, despite the chief investigating officer at the time claiming the murderer was 'still detectable'. Over 30 years later, the case of the Jolly Farmer remains unsolved and is still an open investigation with a reward for information.

The pub was rebuilt shortly after and Arthur continued his position as landlord. There were no further attacks and no new information that surfaced. Arthur sold the pub in 2003.

The Jolly Farmer still exists to this day under new management and holds annual Christmas celebrations. It is still the centre of the village of Blacknest but attracts people from all over Hampshire for its good food and better beer.

Richard Dean suffered incurable burns to his entire body, with a quarter of the burns being severe. He now lives on the Isle of Wight, an island to the south of Hampshire. On top of his physical scars, he was left with mental scars that remind him daily of what happened one Christmas in 1989.

Few drinkers at the pub nowadays are aware of the history that created their comforting drinking hole but someone, somewhere knows the truth of what happened that night.

All that remains of the original Jolly Farmer is a small, round garden, developed on top of the original site. It would be a discomforting twist of fate, if the killer returned each Christmas to drink in the very pub he once destroyed, on top of the very ruins that ended a life.

Gentleman Hacker

A crowd of scientists gathered in London for the first public demonstration of the wireless telegram system, only for a British magician to tap the signal and become the world's first hacker.

L ong gone are the days of using telegrams to send messages across great distances, we're fortunate enough in the digital age to be able to send emails or even texts across the world in a matter of micro-seconds.

In the early 20th Century, things weren't that simple. Telegrams started out in the telegraph age when telecommunication consisted of short messages transmitted by hand over the telegraph wire. They were sent between telegraph services; companies that delivered messages to the recipients.

Charged by the amount of words in the message, telegrams consisted of abbreviations with no punctuation, and minimal words. The very first telegram to be sent was from Orville Wright, on 17th December 1903, about the first powered air flight.

'*Success four flights Thursday morning all against twenty one mile wind started from Level with engine power alone average speed through air thirty one miles longest 57 seconds inform Press home Christmas.*'

Six months earlier, in June 1903, when the telegram system was being showcased in front of eminent individuals and the public in London, someone hacked the network – and insulted the Italian scientist Guglielmo Marconi, who was conducting the test.

Marconi's demonstration

We don't often think of hackers as top-hat wearing men born in the 19th Century but the similarities in the way security hackers are used hasn't really changed much since then. The systems and capabilities we have now are vastly different but they still need to be security tested.

Most hackers as we think of them nowadays, are mostly security experts, who look for flaws in company systems, or in the development of new software. And in 1903, things were not much different.

Though computers didn't exist, avenues of communication did, in the same way modern-day companies are protecting their digital footprint, so did olden-day companies wish to protect their communication lines.

Guglielmo Marconi was a Nobel Prize winning Italian scientist, born in 1874 Bologna, who is known as the inventor of radio. He pioneered long distance radio transmission and developed the very first wireless telegraph system using electromagnetic waves – as dot/dashes of the Morse code.

On that summers day in 1903, some of the world's leading scientists and members of the public were gathered in the lecture hall of the Royal Institution in London, ready to showcase the new Telegram system to the world. Marconi was waiting 300 miles away on a hill in Cornwall, ready to send a message to the eager onlookers.

The system had undergone immense testing, and back in 1901, Marconi had sent the first wireless signals across the Atlantic. Now it was time to show the public it worked, to dispel rumours that the wireless telegraph was unsafe. But someone else had other ideas.

Diddling the public

Moments before the demonstration was about to begin, the equipment kicked into life and began tapping out a message, which shocked the onlookers – and the scientists. At first, the word RATS was repeated over and over again. Then, the telegram got personal.

As the scientists gawped in confusion, a message came over the system that said; 'there was a young fellow of Italy, who diddled the public quite prettily.' Then it is claimed the message continued to rant but no record of it exists beyond the line above.

Being 300 miles away, Marconi was unaware of the intrusion, and continued with the demonstration, but the damage had already been done. When Marconi found out, he was furious.

His very public demonstration had been hacked – or tapped, as was the slang of the day, and the hacker had personally attacked him. Marconi had promised confidential communication channels sent on a frequency that could not have been intercepted.

Someone had tapped into the Royal Institution using strong enough wireless signals to interfere with the equipment's electric arc discharge lamp. But who could have pulled off such an extraordinary feat?

Enter British magician and inventor, Nevil Maskelyne.

Scientific vandalism

Born in 1863, Nevil was a descendant of a long line of British illusionists and inventors. He had been following Marconi's work and wireless technology for some time, purely for the purposes of incorporating it into his magic shows.

He would use Morse code during his shows to communicate with his assistant and team behind the stage, to pull off tricks that wowed his audience. In a book about his mostly unrecorded life, there is a story that he was able to send a radio message from the ground to a hot-air balloon, using equipment he had invented himself.

While Nevil was developing his own wireless system, Marconi managed to get broad patents for the technology, which meant Nevil couldn't develop his systems further. Yet, it wasn't Nevil's idea to hack the demonstration, it was at the request of the British-owned Eastern Telegraph Company.

They were worried the Marconi system wasn't as confidential as it was claimed to be and were aggrieved at having spent a fortune laying cables meant for the previous wired telegraphic system. Hearing of Nevil's work, they commissioned him to prove that Marconi's technology had flaws.

Nevil invented a 25-metre radio antenna that he used to intercept Marconi's test signals. On the day of the demonstration, he used the antenna and signal to taunt Marconi at his demonstration.

Gentleman hacker

An investigation followed where Marconi publicly requested people to unmask the criminal who had gone against all codes of science to ruin his life's work – and mock him! It didn't take long because Nevil was proud of what he had done and admitted to it.

He wrote a letter to a newspaper claiming his intention was to unmask Marconi and reveal the flaws within the so-called private communication system. He ended the letter saying it was for the common good of all mankind.

For many months and years that followed, Marconi persisted that Nevil was an insult to science and should have been arrested for his crimes. However, as with many hackers today, he was commissioned to find flaws in a new technology – which he did.

Marconi went on to win the 1909 Nobel Prize in Physics with Karl Ferdinand Braun for their contributions to the development of wireless telegraphy. In 1931, he set up Vatican Radio for Pope Pius XI, six years before his death in 1937.

Nevil went on to continue his illustrious career in magic, wrote several books on the subject, and died peacefully in 1924. The two men's paths were forever entwined, and due to their rivalry, it is perhaps no surprise that the first hacking in history was used by a Brit to send an insult.

Look for more in the Orrible British True Crime Series!

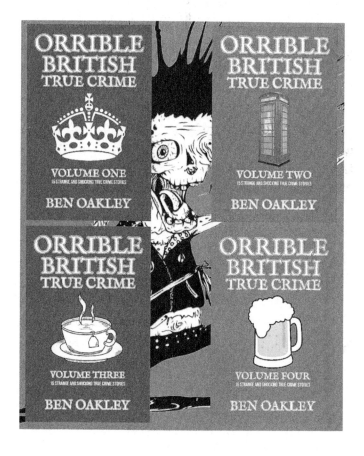

OUT NOW!

For bibliographies, citations, true crime blog posts, more true crime books, and more information on new releases for your collection, head on over to www.benoakley.co.uk